M000306599

Advance Praise for *Nightingales:*
True Stories of Escape, Hope, and Resilience

"Exploding stereotypes and false assumptions, Syrian refugees and migrants tell their own stories in this unique collection. Mimi Melkonian has done a great service by soliciting, compiling, and translating records that communicate the intimate and varied realities of the Syrian migration."

—Todd Fine, President, Washington Street Historical Society

"Since the 2011 Arab Spring, a set of complex geopolitical moves and failure in leadership extended the conflict in Syria, and displaced thousands of Syrians as refugees and immigrants in the Middle East, Europe, and beyond.

In *Nightingales*, Mimi Melkonian sets out to change our perception about Syria and Syrian refugees. She introduces us to resilient Syrians who left Syria to seek sanctuary in other countries—despite all odds, they managed to thrive. Melkonian captures the rich cultural traditions of Syrians while sharing the painful journeys of the recent refugees and their adjustments in their new homelands.

Readers are introduced to refugee artists, athletes, educators, and homemakers who must look ahead, leverage their talents, and establish themselves thousands of miles away from home.

Nightingales celebrates refugees and highlights the richness of their talents and contributions to their new homeland. I highly recommend this book."

—Ani Kharajian, President,
Armenian International Women's Association
Senior Portfolio Director, Executive Education, Harvard Business School
Granddaughter of Armenian Genocide survivors and an immigrant

"A seminal accomplishment. Mimi Melkonian, herself the daughter of Armenian forced migrant heritage, narrates the path of individuals fleeing danger and despair, holding onto little more than hope to steer their destiny.

Essential reading, *Nightingales* is a mastery of what becoming a refugee entails, and testament that no one chooses exile. Beautifully written, every chapter details the arduous journey of dreams morphing into reality. Melkonian crafts each story with eloquence and empathy, taking the reader into lives they would never otherwise know."

—Susan Hanna-Wicht, President, Global Language Project

Nightingales

TRUE STORIES OF ESCAPE, HOPE, AND RESILIENCE

Cráter Publishers, LLC
Ediciones del Crater
New York City

Published by:
Cráter Publishers, LLC
Ediciones del Cráter
New York City

Series: *Contemporary World Issues,* Volume 1
For information, contact: delcrater@gmail.com
Visit us at www.delcraterediciones.com

ISBN: 978-0-9971753-3-2

Publisher logo by Angela Ocaña (all rights reserved)
Cover design by Gagica Albian
Book design by Summer R. Morris (www.SumoDesignStudio.com)
Publishing services by Second City Publishing Services, LLC
(www.secondcitypublishing.com)

NIGHTINGALES

True Stories of Escape, Hope, and Resilience

DEDICATION

Dedicated to all Syrian migrants,
forced migrants, and refugees.

In memory of my parents,
Hagop Melkonian
and Angèle Apoyan.

CONTENTS

INTRODUCTION

My parents were forced migrants.

Forced to leave Adana, in contemporary Southern Turkey in the context of the Armenian Genocide, my father came to Lebanon in 1921. According to my grandparents, my father's aunt, Hoki, had been a translator for an American missionary at what is now known as Tarsus American College. While translating some documents, she discovered that the Turks were preparing to attack and round up Armenians in Adana and Tarsus. She informed her sister (my grandmother), and my grandparents both prepared to flee immediately. Leaving everything behind, they headed to the port at Mersin on the southern coast and took a ship to Beirut. My father, at age five, his parents, his twin siblings, and his eldest brother all left, never to return.

They took with them only their fears and their memories. Out of eighty-five of my father's family members, only seven survived. The rest were massacred, along with a million-and-a-half other innocent Armenians. Walking to the port, then sailing from

Mersin to a Syrian port city, and then riding on a cattle train via Damascus into Lebanon, they arrived in Beirut and settled in a quarantine camp. They did not speak Arabic, nor did they carry any possessions, but they were thankful to have survived. After growing up in Beirut, my father did well and became the chief of construction for one of the largest shipbuilding and repair companies in the Middle East, Polycarbos Dimitrius, Poldim Works. He managed more than two hundred skilled construction workers, both men and women. My father, in turn, helped many young Armenian orphans start new lives and families after meeting them at Poldim Works. He received an honorary medal from King Constantine II of Greece for his innovative achievements in shipbuilding. He established a trade union in Lebanon, and for the first time, workers were granted eight-hour workdays instead of being forced to labor for extended hours with little compensation. His love of music and violin-playing brightened our weekly family dinner evenings. He had five children and lived a comfortable life in Beirut, Lebanon.

My mother had her own forced migration story.

In 1915, her parents fled Siverek to Adana, the major city of south-central Anatolia. (Siverek is an ancient city dating to the Armenian Urartian period of 1000 BC). The family lived in Adana until 1921, and my mother was born in 1920 or 1921. She was still a baby when her parents had to flee again, this time from Adana due to the massacres conducted by the Turkish government. Like my father's family, they took the boat from Mersin and arrived in Beirut. My mother grew up in Beirut and eventually started teaching at a day school, where she organized theatrical productions in which she also acted. She donated part of her salary to help build a school and a church for Armenian children. She was also an active member in the Armenian General Benevolent Union and helped coordinate scholarships for Armenians to pursue higher education in Beirut. In 1908, when my mother's brother was not yet even a teenager, he fled to the United States from Mersin. He never saw his parents again. Fifty-seven years later, my mother tracked him down, and they met again in Philadelphia.

My parents worked hard to give us the security they never had, something that forced migrants consider vital.

Under present-day international crises, forced migrants face different circumstances, and global politics have also changed. Still, forced migrants continue to flee war and persecution. They lose all of their sources of security, having abandoned everything familiar— family, friends, culture, home, and work. Sometimes traveling in unsafe conditions by sea and land, they risk their lives to reach safety. The questions asked when making desperate escapes are the same for all forced migrants around the globe: Where should I go? How can I eat? Where should I sleep? Where can I work? Whom can I trust? Where can I find work?

The war in Syria has created a massive crisis of forced migration. The divisions within the Arab world and the Middle East have prevented an adequate humanitarian response. Ian Bremmer, the president and founder of the Eurasia Group, has stated that we are living in a "leaderless world," with no capacity to respond to crisis.[1] The United States itself seems to have lost much of the moral leadership that many have traditionally relied on. Syrian refugees

---

[1] Bremmer, Ian. "The Era of American Global Leadership Is Over. Here's What Comes Next," *Time*, December 19, 2016; http://time.com/4606071/american-global-leadership-is-over/

and migrants were dehumanized during the U.S. presidential election in 2016. They were also cited as a motivating factor for British citizens choosing to leave the European Union in 2016. Sadly, despite the demonization in Western politics, Syrian forced migrants are largely the victims of extremist organizations. Very few are terrorists themselves.

Having experienced the Civil War in Lebanon (1975-1990) as a teenager, I have enormous empathy for the victims of the war in Syria. The Lebanese war brought untold difficulties and changed our lives completely. We all lived day-to-day, hoping and praying the war would end the next morning.

In 1978, my family was internally displaced and had to leave our mountain house in Bois De Boulogne and head to the Bekaa Valley town of Anjar. Like many people who have experienced war, I had many traumatizing experiences that I still find difficult to verbalize.

Although I cannot be considered a forced migrant myself, in 2001 I left Lebanon and migrated to the United States. In Lebanon, I was an accomplished pianist who taught at the Lebanese National Higher Conservatory of Music. I had toured many European countries and the United States and entered my students in various international piano competitions. However, after migrating with my children, I found it difficult to lead a creative life as before, due to the responsibilities of earning a living and raising my children in the United States. Therefore, one motive for this collection was to assist other creative people, now migrants, in their efforts to support themselves and tell their stories.

As the war in Syria continued to worsen, I could not help but think about people's experiences through the lens of my own.

Living in the United States, I read in popular media about how Syrian refugees and forced migrants navigated their escapes and attempted to build new lives. On Arabic social media, I also discovered other agonizing stories that would never be shown on television. I realized that Syrian civilians were writing and telling their true stories.

As a teacher of Arabic language, I was particularly attuned to the misconceptions about Middle Easterners and Syrians held among Westerners. Increasingly, I wanted to counter these somehow and help tell the true stories of Syrian migrants.

Two years ago, a visit to Berlin, Germany helped me understand the authentic experience of the Syrian refugee. My tragic and depressing outlook began to find some strands of hope for the future. In Berlin, milling around in my hotel lobby and walking through the streets, I constantly heard Arabic and I ended up speaking with many Syrians. Asking them a battery of questions about their journeys, I was fascinated at how many of these people, who had never traveled before in their lives and had not spoken a word of German, were now living in Germany with permits to work and live independently. I observed the courage and determination of the Syrian migrants through what they were able to accomplish in a short period. These achievements were clearly advanced through an ethic of community. Having survived and then living a free life had made them more selfless human beings. They helped each other as a rule, and if a stranger asked for assistance, they would not hesitate to give advice and help. This ethic of selflessness is something that I had also witnessed among the Armenian Genocide survivors that I knew in Lebanon.

As I began to appreciate and notice this ethic, I observed it on social media, on Facebook and Instagram, with so many Syrians helping each other, even if they were strangers. For example, if one wanted to find how to travel in Europe, Syrians would pose questions on social media and people who had already fled would post answers. Information on finding the most honest and safest smugglers, as they call them, was discussed on social media.

After I returned from Berlin in 2016, I decided to develop a book project of interviews of Syrian migrants. On television, most stories of Syrian refugees and forced migrants show people living in camps, who are presented and sensationalized as uneducated, dirty, and hopeless. Without denying the difficulties that such people face, I wanted to tell stories of Syrians who were determined to build successful lives in the West. Many Americans are unaware that Syria, as well as my home country of Lebanon, was filled with many well-educated people who most certainly had the ability to succeed anywhere through hard work. A number of such Syrians have told their stories on social media, but I decided to collect and share some of the most inspiring ones.

Through connections made on social media and through personal contacts, I invited around twenty-five individuals to do recorded interviews, which we agreed that I would transcribe into a narrative and send back for their review. Some declined and did not want their stories published, fearing that their loved ones in Syria could be harmed; others felt their lives and stories should be kept private. Sixteen people agreed, many of them artists already accustomed to telling their stories to public audiences. I attempted as much as possible to retain their voice and use their actual language in literal translation.

I personally interviewed every speaker in this volume. Their original stories were provided in Arabic, Armenian, or Turkish, with a few in English. I recorded each story and then transcribed and translated the recording into English. When I performed the interviews, I was a total stranger to all of them, except to Talar Dekrmanjian and Lena Tavitian. I knew Talar from the International Piano and Voice Competition in Sicily, Italy, which I judged in 1999. I knew Lena from Beirut, where we both attended the Armenian General Benevolent Union's Yervant Demirdjian School in Zarif, Beirut, and since we were cousins, we stayed in touch.

All other interviewees I met virtually. I used Facebook, WhatsApp, Instagram, and Twitter to learn their stories and then contact them.

Some readers might ask why these stories do not seek more to project the inner emotions and traumas of the interviewees. Instead, my interviews were focused more on the mechanics of how these people were able to build new lives in the West and share their Syrian identity with the world, often through their art or daily life. Some interviewees are famous Syrian artists, and others ordinary civilians. While a number of the artists have attempted to explain the experience of the Syrian refugee or war victim through their artwork, in these interviews, I sought more to understand their daily, basic challenges of life as lived, rather than how they are expressed in their artistic practice. Even though artists have fame and have the means to express their emotions with a variety of tools, at the end of the day, they still experience the same practical difficulties as everyone else.

To be a total stranger and perform an interview on such emotional subjects was not easy, especially because in our Middle Eastern culture we find it difficult to share our inner emotions with strangers. In general, if you ask a Middle Easterner, "How are you, today?" the answer will be: "Thank God, I am fine." It could be that the person has many worries, but the outlook towards life is always to be thankful and hopeful for a better day according to God's will. And perhaps, this region of the world that has seen the rise and fall of so many empires and civilizations, and so many wars and peace agreements, has made its inhabitants look at life with a focus on what they can do immediately to improve their situation and not dwell on their traumas of the past.

In addition to forced migrants (people who leave their home country because they have no other choice) and proper "refugee" stories (a defined category in international law theoretically entitled to entry and support), I included several stories of regular Syrian migrants. Migrants are those who leave their home country voluntarily in search of better economic opportunities or to pursue higher education abroad. A number of the Syrians I interviewed had been studying abroad or had decided to migrate before the war. Once the war broke out, they could no longer return to Syria. Their parents, siblings, and close family members became scattered all over the world. While such migrants may not have undergone the same traumatic experiences as forced migrants or refugees, many of them still suffered because they could not unite with their parents or other loved ones. Many live their lives with hopes of uniting with their loved ones, while many others have lost loved ones.

I would also like to stress that the Syrians who are living in camps are struggling and surviving in their own way—by working in the camps or attempting to bring the normality of school and weddings into this environment. They also are survivors, and they hope one day that they will be able to return to their homeland. There are some excellent and respectful documentaries that try to give voice to the hundreds of thousands of people in Syrian refugee camps.

Despite feeling the pain of this ongoing tragedy, I wanted to share voices of hope and survival in this book. These authentic stories remind me of my parents. Although these individuals have lived through traumatic circumstances that many people may not want to hear, and which they themselves may not be prepared to process fully, they are attempting to tell their truths. Keats' nightingale sings of divine truth. Syrians are still attempting to tell the basic truth of their journeys as forced migrants and refugees. For the time being, until this crisis is resolved, these stories of truth nevertheless signal human resilience and hope.

My mother, Angèle Apoyan (far right, back row), and my aunt, Maryam Melkonian (far left, back row) with the school principle Baron Vahan. Circa 1935. My mother was teaching at Giligian School, in Beirut. All the children were children of Armenian Genocide survivors. None have shoes on their feet.

ACKNOWLEDGMENTS

In gratitude to Dr. Jaime Gonzalez-Ocaña for getting me moving on publishing this book, and for his kind encouragement along the way; to Dr. Kevin Donnelly, for his insightful comments; and to the sixteen interviewees for giving their time in conducting live interviews or answering questions by email.

Particular thanks to the cover artist, Albian Gagica.

My heartfelt appreciation also goes to Cynthia Zaven for giving me her time to talk and discuss nuances from Beirut, Rome, Amsterdam, and Paris.

Lastly, and most importantly, I would like to express warm thanks to my husband, Howard Aibel; my children, Julie-Anne and Marc Baghadjian; my niece, Karina Melkonian; and my brothers and sisters for their unfailing love, encouragement, and support. I thank all my colleagues, friends, and family members who helped and guided me in this work.

Where the nightingale doth sing
Not a senseless, tranced thing,
But divine melodious truth;
Philosophic numbers smooth;
Tales and golden histories
Of heaven and its mysteries

Ode (Bards of Passion and of Mirth), 17–22
—John Keats

CHAPTER 1

The Arabic Library in Berlin
Muhannad Qaiconie (Germany)

*This interview was the longest one since the interviewee
had such a traumatic and long journey from Syria to
Berlin. Many Syrians fleeing Syria made this journey,
and I was fortunate to have Mr. Qaiconie recount his
experience of his own journey from east to west.*

Muhannad Qaiconie was born and raised in Aleppo before enrolling as a student of English literature at the University of Latakia (now known as Tishreen University). He joined the resistance at the outbreak of fighting in 2011, and in 2013, after being detained by government forces, was forced to flee the country. His harrowing journey of migration from Turkey to Germany, with stops along the way to make money, lasted over two years. Through his ambitious outreach to others and the kindness that others showed toward him, he founded Baynetna, an Arabic-German library and cultural center, to promote intercultural understanding. His story has become a global inspiration. Muhannad is majoring in politics and ethics at Bard College Berlin.

—◄•►—

Growing up in Syria was a dead end. The dictatorship, the repressive regime, and the socioeconomic situation prevented me from flourishing there. The Assad regime addressed this situation through a campaign of propaganda, which upheld ideas such as, "Living outside your country is difficult," or, "Leaving your country will reduce your opportunities." The common message was that everyone should stay in his own country. On the other hand, after receiving your education, there were no jobs. As a result, everyone was forced to work a different position than they were trained for, and received a minimal salary. One couldn't plan his or her future and was obliged to stay and live in Syria.

It is hard for me to speak about my good and bad memories because I do not have any good ones. All I remember is being part of a generation that could not find jobs or opportunities to build a future and be successful. I have always worked hard at improving my situation and taking chances to get ahead in life. The Syrian government propaganda tried to force and convince us to stay in Syria. Before fleeing Syria, I had never traveled in my life, never lived alone, never been encouraged to live alone. This kind of propaganda affected me. Even when my friends left for the Gulf in search of job opportunities, I argued and tried to convince them to stay in Syria.

When the civil war started in 2011, I joined the resistance, and by 2013, after being detained by government forces, I was forced to flee the country. During this time, I took part in demonstrations and left college, where I was majoring in English literature. I thought, even if I graduated, what job opportunities are there for me? Become a teacher? Or get any other poorly compensated job? So, I left college and became a witness to the regime's brutal atrocities. Centuries-old architectural masterpieces were destroyed. Bustling marketplaces (souqs) disappeared. Hospitals, schools, mosques, churches, homes, and heritage sites were pummeled into dust—including our house. Many neighborhoods turned into ghost towns. Scenes of apocalyptic devastation were brought to Aleppo, Homs (a city in western Syria), Raqqa (located on the northeast bank of the Euphrates), and Deir ez-Zor (a city in eastern Syria).

I decided to leave Syria for Lebanon, even though I knew about the difficulties I would face there as well. I had to help my divorced mother and two sisters with their daily expenses. I was twenty-five and it was my first time traveling out of Syria. My journey started in Aleppo; we traveled via Damascus and finally made our way into Lebanon. When we arrived at Chtaura (a town in Lebanon located halfway on the Damascus-to-Beirut highway), the militias stopped the bus and started interrogating the passengers. We were all frightened and at a loss for words. We were asked questions such as, "Who is with the revolution and who is against it?" At that moment, I started to think and said to myself, "This did not happen to me in Syria. Now that I am away from the shelling and the war, I have to face these unknown militias and answer them." If I told them that I was with the revolution, they could either kill me or let me remain free, depending on which side they were on. I did not know what to say. Ultimately, I just wanted to survive. I kept quiet. At that point, one of the militia members asked, "Where will you stay in Lebanon?"

A man spoke up: "I am going to Dahieh." Dahieh is a suburb in south Lebanon where its inhabitants are Shia.

The militia immediately responded, "So, you are against the revolution."

The gentleman responded, "No, I have a family there, and must join them."

Right then I realized the militia were with the revolution. The interrogations went on and on. All passengers were forced to state where they were going. Each person was heading to a different town in Lebanon that represented a stance that was either with or against the Syrian regime.

In the end, they announced: "If you do not have a house to stay in, please come with us. We are with Saad al-Hariri (the prime minister of Lebanon, a Sunni politician) and we will provide you with a place to stay and help you out."

No one left the bus. We all stayed silent and wanted to move on and arrive at our destinations.

Three of my friends and I made it to Beirut. We met a friend there and were able to stay at his place. The next day, I left for Jbeil (Byblos, an ancient city in northern Lebanon). Jbeil is a Christian town. I preferred staying there over a Shia or Sunni town. I knew that the Christians were with the opposition forces and were helping Syrians who had fled the country. My friends joined me, and five of us rented a house and found work in building construction. Our rent was four hundred dollars per month, and we each made fifty dollars per day. We worked for three weeks and were able to pay our bills, send money home, and keep some savings.

After three weeks, I started to look for a different job. I began delivering food. At first, I did not know how to ride a motorcycle, but the shop owner taught me. One day, when I delivered pizza to a hairdresser's shop, the hairdresser offered me a job. I did not know anything about hair care. The hairdresser promised to teach me how to help him in his parlor. I agreed and started to work for him. He also let me know that his brother was a carpenter and I could sleep in his workshop, instead of staying at my place and paying rent. I agreed, and started working for him.

Life was not easy. One day, when I returned to sleep at the workshop, I couldn't find my clothes. A neighbor, Noel, had taken my clothes to wash them. Since my arrival in Lebanon, this was the first time I got help with my wash! Noel, a Lebanese Christian, was a religious person. He offered to let me stay at his house and spend evenings with his family. He had a statue of the Virgin Mary in his shop, prayed every morning when he arrived, and on Sundays went to church. I started to go to church with him, and then we visited sacred sites and prayed there too. People were kind to me in Jbeil. I received help from strangers wherever I went. I was able to stay in touch with my family in Syria through the internet. There were times when their internet would go down for several days, and I would get anxious. Once service was restored, I would have peace of mind.

As time went on, I started to realize that the war in Syria would not end soon, and I must have a long-term plan for my future. I needed to start my life all over again and help my family also leave

Syria. Just existing in Lebanon was not a solution. I found out from others that going to Turkey, and then continuing to Europe, was the way to start a decent and safe life.

I had two hundred dollars on me, and I paid 175 dollars of that amount to take a boat to Turkey. I arrived in Mersin, found a hotel to stay in, but did not have enough money for a night's stay. I spent the night outside. The next morning, I started to look for work as a hairdresser. I met a woman who could not speak Arabic, but with body language, we were able to communicate. She called her friends in Gaziantep who spoke Arabic and asked them to translate our conversation. She decided to offer me a job at her salon and agreed to pay me fifteen Turkish liras per day.

I was so happy, I went to a hotel and made the arrangements to stay there for a month. I was able to speak English with the hotel owner and explain my situation. He was a kind gentleman. Although the rent was fifty Turkish liras per day, which exceeded my salary of fifteen Turkish liras, he allowed me to stay. He considered me a guest in his hotel and asked me to pay as much as I could. Ebru, my hairdresser boss, offered the hotel owner free services at her parlor, and I could take a shower and wash my clothes at her place whenever I needed to.

I started to work, and after three weeks she invited me to her house to play backgammon and cards. Eventually, I stayed in her house for a year and a half and thus was able to save money and send it home to my mom. After some time in Turkey, I started to think about going back to college. I tried, but it did not work. It was at this point that I began to think that it was time to move on. I felt I must leave for Europe and try to go back to college. It was true that I had been able to save some money because I was staying in my employer's house, but if I were to have my family join me, it would be impossible for us to live together. While many people in Turkey were kind to me, this was not enough for me to get established and support my family. So, I thought of Europe, and more specifically, Germany. I started to network with Syrians about how I could begin my journey. Eventually, I decided to leave Turkey from Mersin and sail to Greece.

I was afraid of the sea, and all the stories we were hearing about capsizing boats and dinghies only made my fears worse. Money was also an issue. To make the crossing from Turkey to Greece affordable, I bought a small boat with friends and decided to depart from Edirne (a city close to Turkey's borders with Greece and Bulgaria), where we could sail on the Maritsa River instead of crossing the Aegean Sea. As three friends together, we planned to travel from Turkey to Greece, and then to Bulgaria. Unfortunately, our attempt was short-lived. The Turkish Army caught us and put us in a camp for two days. My friends were afraid to try again. Only my classmate Nasser and I decided to take a boat. However, this time we decided to cross the Aegean Sea from Izmir with smugglers as many other Syrians did.

We started to study the map and searched social media to find a smuggler. We learned about some Afghans who had bought a boat by themselves and crossed the Aegean Sea. Their method was to enter Greek territorial waters. They rowed the boat into the territorial waters and waited for the police to come and take them into custody. These smugglers usually charged one thousand dollars per person for a boat with fifty people. So they brought in fifty thousand dollars, while the cost of the vessel was just five thousand dollars.

I found a smuggler on Facebook who was reliable. Usually, on social media, people would comment whether their journey with a smuggler was successful or not. This was a kind of statistical data that gave you an idea of how reliable a particular smuggler was. I deduced from the comments that I could trust him, and it was evident that most of his dinghies had made it to the Greek islands. I paid him one thousand dollars, as did forty-two other passengers. Nasser and I were ready to sail.

At 10 a.m. one bright morning, the smuggler told us it was time to start the journey. I don't swim, and was terrified. Initially, I thought he wasn't serious, and wondered why we weren't crossing the Aegean Sea at night. I was horrified by the idea of sailing in the daytime. It was my second attempt at sailing, and all my hopes depended on this journey. Our smuggler scanned the Aegean Sea through his binoculars and then signaled that we should board.

We all put on life jackets. I was still very nervous. I had seen on the news that many migrants had drowned in the Aegean Sea as they tried to reach Greece. We all wrapped our cell phones in layers of sealed plastic bags. Packed tightly, all forty-three of us and an Algerian who steered the dinghy started our journey towards one of the Greek islands. After more than two hours of sailing, we approached an island. We were packed so tightly that I lost all feeling in my legs. We were all very stressed and wondered if we could make it safely to the shore. Suddenly, the Algerian took out a knife and stuck it into the rubber part of the boat. Everyone started to panic. Escaping air hissed from the boat, and water gushed into it. People started to scream and push each other in their rush to escape the sinking boat. We did not understand why he had done this. Apparently, in order to ensure our arrival to Greece, the Algerian sank the boat so that the approaching Greek Coast Guard vessel could not force us back into Turkish waters. We all managed to make it to the rocky shore. I immediately unwrapped my phone and checked to see if we had indeed made it to Greece. I opened the Google Maps application and found out that we were in Greece, and on safe land. We were all happy and joyful that we had made it, and started taking selfies. I thought I had passed the most difficult part of my journey, but very soon found out that was not the case.

We had landed on the tiny island of Agathonisi and I quickly realized that life on the islands was appalling. The Greek authorities did not have the means to keep up with the relentless wave of arrivals. They had to register each migrant and issue renewable papers to stay in Greece for six months. Only Syrians had this privilege. The other migrants, such as the Iraqis, Eritreans, Afghans, and Moroccans, were only allowed to stay one month. Many migrants had to wait weeks in the camps before receiving their documents. Even though some islands had official reception centers to provide migrants with shelter and food, these places were overcrowded. On some of the islands, the new arrivals were left to survive on their own. Chaos was the norm.

On the island, we went to the police in Agathonisi and spent one night in jail. But when it became too crowded, the police moved us outside, and we slept on the ground. A new group of refugees arrived that day and walked into the jail. After two and a half days, during which the police fed us only once, we were sent to Sámos and waited a week for our papers.

At first, we did not know what the procedures in the camp were, but refugees who had arrived before us started to give us some details. We knew that Syrian refugees had priority over all other nationalities. Syrians could have their papers issued and stay in Greece for six months. People started to provide false information about their citizenship in order to stay in Greece for six months. Aware of what was going on, the Greek authorities began to ask personal questions like, "Where do you live in Syria; in which town?" "Is this a Syrian currency?" "Can you sing the national anthem of Syria?"

Children who were eighteen years old or younger could send for their parents once they entered a European Union country. As a result, many families sent their kids to Greece so that they could then follow them into Europe. These children stayed at a separate camp. Some non-Syrian adults were lying and saying that they were eighteen. There was no proof because there were no birth certificates. Everyone in the refugee camp wanted to stay in a European Union country.

Some non-Syrian refugees would say that they were siblings of a Syrian one, which was of course, untrue. The police took hold of this situation and started to interrogate both so-called siblings, asking questions like, "Give us your aunt's name, the names of your family members, where you went to school, where you lived, the names of your best friends." If both so-called siblings gave the same answers, they were given papers to stay in Greece. Otherwise, they had to leave within a month. Incredibly, many people prepared well for this interrogation, and they passed!

People wanted to have a new chance to live in a safe environment and have the opportunity to work and grow.

The news of these success stories traveled quickly. Soon, many who were living in Syria, Turkey, and camps in Jordan, Lebanon, Afghanistan, Morocco, and Iraq expected to land on the islands, have their papers done in a week, and then travel to other E.U. countries. Facebook and social media helped spread the word, and a sudden influx of refugees started to pour onto the islands. I left the camp in Sámos before significant numbers of refugees arrived. The Greek authorities did not have the means to cope with the needs of the refugees. Even though refugees were trying to help each other, they still had to wait while Greek authorities processed them sequentially. As a result, the situations in the camps became horrendous.

Muhannad's journey from Turkey to Germany
(Credit: Mimi Melkonian, mapchart.net)

I stayed at the Sámos camp for one week. Living there was like living in a ghetto. The refugee camp had numerous shelters that were divided by nationality: Syrian, Iraqi, Afghani, Moroccan, Eritrean. Each shelter had its own facilities. These groups of people did not interact except when using the facilities because one shelter was the only one with hot water, another was the only one with a bathroom, and another had just one toilet. People started to go to the other shelters to wash or use the bathroom. In the morning, there would be a long line to go to the toilet, or to wash up. Fights were inevitable. It was mayhem living under these unhealthy conditions. Food was served twice a day, at breakfast and dinner. Breakfast consisted of one piece of bread with butter, jam, and a cup of coffee with milk. The bunk beds provided could not accommodate everyone, so some refugees were forced to sleep on the floor. Newcomers slept on the floor until a bunk bed occupier left the camp. During the day, we sat and told each other stories about how we fled from Syria to Greece, and shared tips about how to survive in the camp.

We learned that if you entered the refugee camp on Sunday, you would leave the next Sunday. Everyone was planning how and where to go. Some had already paid the smugglers seven thousand dollars to get from Turkey to Germany. The smugglers were waiting for them. Some wanted to leave and travel on foot because they did not have any money. We were always checking social media, especially Facebook, to see how others before us were making it to Europe. Everyone shared their plans.

Nasser and I decided to leave together, but wanted to have a few more people with us. We met five other refugees who wanted to join us. One of the five was a young teenager. He was alone and should have stayed in the camp because he was considered an unaccompanied minor. A stranger volunteered to pose as his father, and told the authorities that this young boy was his son. In a week's time, they released five of us, along with others. We were transferred to a large boat that set sail to Athens. Each one of us paid fifty dollars to get on the ship. We started sailing and as we arrived at different islands, new passengers joined, while others disembarked. After twelve hours, we arrived at Athens.

Early the next morning, five of us took the train to Thessaloniki and then the bus to Evzonoi, which is on the border of Greece and Macedonia. The bus left us off before reaching Evzonoi, so we had to walk for thirty kilometers (about nineteen miles) towards the border, a journey that took us about eight hours. It was rainy, muddy, and our route was often blocked by rivers too deep to cross by walking. We eventually arrived at Bitola, Macedonia, where the police arrested us. I tried to bribe them, but this was a bad move. The police were upset with me, and I got handcuffed. Other police officers beat an older man in our group with their batons. We were all sent back to the border and ordered to cross back into Greece. The police officer told me: "Don't come back, or next time I will beat you to death."

We returned to Hotel Hara in Evzoni (on the Greece-Macedonian border). I became ill and stayed in bed for two days. Doctors Without Borders took care of me. Although we were afraid, we were determined to cross the border once more. Nasser told me we shouldn't go, but I insisted on trying again.

Hotel Hara had European guests who had arrived by car, as well as the refugees who intended to cross the border. It was a gloomy place where people rested before continuing their journey. Migrants slept in the parking lot and surrounding land. The rooms were all occupied. Laundry hung on every fence. There was always a group of journalists hanging around, covering the migrant story. One journalist I met, Kristen Chick, wrote about my journey, and followed me until I arrived in Germany. Her articles helped me to connect with people from all over the world, people who helped me throughout my journey.

Nasser and I decided to cross the border for the second time. This time we took a heavily trafficked path north of Thessaloniki. Unfortunately, after hours of walking, we got arrested by the police at Gevgelija, fifteen kilometers (about nine miles) from Hotel Hara. We had decided to take the bus at Gevgelija instead of walking the rest of the way. I did not notice that the police station was opposite the bus station. Many people like us were waiting to take the bus, the police came and arrested all of us, and again we were sent back to the Greek border and forced to reenter Greece. We all walked back to Hotel Hara. We were lucky to end up on the Greek border and not on the Bulgarian one. People who ended up at the Bulgarian border had a difficult time. The Bulgarian police were brutal. They beat up Syrian refugees, and since Bulgaria belonged to the E.U., refugees had to stay in Bulgaria and could not continue their journey to Germany. Syrians did not want to stay in Bulgaria because there were no job opportunities, but once they received their papers they had to end their journey and start living in Bulgaria despite the scarcity of work.

At Hotel Hara, we heard about many horrible stories of migrants crossing Macedonia. The policemen robbed some of the refugees, beat them up, detained many in Skopje, the capital, and kept the refugees in filthy cells. Many crossed the country entirely on foot by following the railroad tracks, and many were killed when hit by trains. Criminal gangs kidnapped refugees and held them for ransom. Our second attempt failed, but Nasser and I decided to try again for the third time.

This time, we decided to travel without the help of a smuggler, and instead used our smartphones with GPS and word of mouth about which path to take. We depended on migrants who had gone before us to advise us through social media links. At Hotel Hara, we formed a group of about one hundred migrants and decided to leave early next morning.

It was dark at 4 a.m. We stuffed our personal belongings into our backpacks. The self-appointed leader of the group gathered the men to discuss security procedures. Women and children would walk in the middle, surrounded by the men. He commanded everyone to turn their phones on silent, insisted that all children be quiet, and that everyone keep together and keep walking. All the men carried tall tree branches to protect the women and the children if we got attacked by gangs.

We crossed wheat fields and entered the forest. Everyone was so silent that the only thing audible was our footsteps in the grass. We spent nearly thirty hours crossing the country, and when we reached the train station to ride north of Belgrade, we heard musicians playing an accordion and a drum. We joined hands and danced the "Dabke" to the music. With all our pain and uncertainty about what was waiting for us, we took advantage of this happy moment.

We planned to go to the next village and hide in the bushes until the train arrived. We knew the train would arrive at 5 a.m. at a specific place. This stop was the one after Evzonoi. It was a small village with no train station, just a small platform. So, we hid and waited until morning. We took the train and paid for our tickets on the train. We all had to pay ten dollars, which was three times the standard fare when converted into Macedonian money. But we had no choice. We got off the train before it arrived at Skopje.

We then got on another train that we planned to disembark before reaching the border with Serbia. We walked toward the border crossing, where there was a station, and we saw some men talking in Turkish. Macedonia has a significant minority population of Turks who live there. Since I had lived in Turkey, I knew how to speak Turkish. We approached them, and I asked them for instructions. The men were very kind. They explained to us how to continue our journey. My Turkish language became a valuable asset. They told us which train to take and where to get off. They also told us about a route that the police do not patrol so that we could be safe. All one hundred of us in the group took the train and made it to Serbia without any problems along the way.

When we left Skopje, we walked in the direction the gentlemen indicated for many hours and got tired. We slept for a couple of hours in the wilderness. It was a long walk. The women were tired, but we continued, took the train, and then walked again to Serbia. It took us around forty-eight hours from Greece to Macedonia to Serbia. Once we were in Serbia, we entered the first village that had a mosque. We washed, bought food and drink, and interacted with the people there. There were many people there who were ready to get out of Serbia. There were taxis and motorcycles, all of which charged fees. They told us they could take us to Belgrade and from there we could get on the train to leave. There were so many of them there, looking to transfer refugees for a fee, and they charged everyone differently. We decided not to pay anything to anyone and go to the Serbian police station instead.

There was a police officer inside the train station. We went in and told them we were from Syria. They agreed to help us and complete our paperwork so that we could leave Serbia on the next train within three days. We waited until the evening, received our papers, and were set to go.

We took the train but were not allowed to sit down. It was a long trip from where we got on to Belgrade. When we got to Belgrade, Serbia's capital, we were all exhausted. We found a hotel and hoped to rest, but we were only allowed to stay in the country for three days. We did not have much time to relax. We needed to think up a plan and leave in the next few hours. We had to keep in mind that we had already lost one day traveling from the village where we were to Belgrade, meaning we only had two more nights left. I started to wonder if I should stay in Serbia and work for a few months, make some money, and then go. But thankfully, a friend from abroad loaned me seven hundred dollars and advised me to leave Serbia. With that money, I started to think about the best way to reach Germany and not end up in Hungary or another European Union country where job opportunities were scarce, and life complicated.

In Serbia, we networked on Facebook and found some smugglers who would help us make it. We got connected with a

Syrian man who had been living in Hungary for thirty years and knew everything about the country. He told us to approach the border at Horgoš at 5 a.m. From Horgoš we had to follow the train tracks and enter Hungary. Horgoš is the last village in Serbia, and he told us that right after entering Hungary, we should make a left and there would be two gas stations. We were then to walk and enter one of these gas stations. There would be a car waiting to drive us to Budapest. The driver required four hundred dollars for the car ride (one hundred dollars for each of us). Everything went smoothly.

In Hungary, there were two border crossing checkpoints, Horgoš and one other. Most of the traffic was heading in the other direction and almost no one was heading in the direction we were. We were lucky: we passed through easily, and from there it was two to three hours to Budapest. The smugglers had dealt with hotel arrangements, so they took us directly there. The next morning, they asked for four hundred dollars per person to get to Austria or five hundred dollars to get to Germany. However, the cost of getting to Austria by train was far cheaper, just twenty dollars. Nasser and I decided to keep traveling by car because we knew that no one would be checking. The two of us paid the one thousand dollars and were driven to the first village in Germany. It took us six or seven hours, but we made it to Passau, Germany. Once there, I called a friend of mine who lived in Bonn. He was a Kurdish guy whose name was Bahri. The two of us grew up together. We lived in the same neighborhood and went to the same school.

Once in Germany, I was still not sure what to do. I was thinking about staying in Germany, or maybe going on to Sweden. I asked

Bahri if I could stay with him for a few days, and possibly go to the police near him, so that I could have the time to decide what to do. He welcomed me and told me I could come to Bonn. After purchasing our tickets, the police stopped us. They spoke to us in German; we did not understand them. They arrested us, gave us a cigarette, and then brought us to the police station. They were very kind to us compared to all the brutality we had found in other countries. As a foreigner, you cannot live in a country without a permit; in Germany that meant going to a refugee shelter, registering, and living there, and then starting your new life. The next day, they sent us to an asylum center. They brought us to a main centralized center at first. Refugees were collected there and then sent out to smaller camps. This central location was in Freyung. Nasser and I shared a room with a balcony and a private bathroom. What a privilege! We had medical exams, had our fingerprints taken, and our papers issued within a short period. After that, Nasser and I separated when we got sent to different camps.

I got sent to a camp near Munich. During that time, I came upon an article in Arabic that had been written by a German journalist. Her name was Ines Kappert. It was originally an article written in German, then translated into Arabic. The article blew me away. I contacted the journalist through Facebook and started to chat with her. She asked me how I was doing and if I needed anything. And of course, I was curious about the Germans, so I asked her for some literature and philosophy books in Arabic because I thought it would be a good way for me to pass the time while I was in the camp. I was not sure if she would be able to find Arabic books in Germany, but Ines told me right away that she could find them. She bought me many books from Amazon, including works by German philosophers and writers translated into Arabic. She got me works by Kafka, Nietzsche, and Patrick Süskind. Additionally, she got me an iPad with internet connectivity, which I had not even asked for. While this communication was going on, she heard that I was in a camp of four hundred refugees that shared one bathroom, and that we had to wait in a long line just to get into the facilities, and told me that I should leave at once.

As refugees, we had the right to leave the camp for a couple of days. Ines put me in touch with a friend of hers, who graciously let me stay at his place. After being there for a week, Ines again put me in contact with another friend, Katharina Enzensberger. She and her husband, Magnus, are both well-known German authors in Munich. They invited me over, and let me stay at their house. Everyone was trying to help me. The house was right there in Munich, and it had a humongous library with thousands of books: I had never seen such a place! They gave me some books in Arabic which were in German initially. Magnus also gave me the book he had written, and he wanted to know my opinion of his work. They were incredibly kind to me, and I found them both to be very humble. I told them my story and how Ines sent me books while I was at the camp. We immediately started talking about German literature. Their house was a real hub of intellectuals: painters, writers, and artists were always passing through.

After some time, Ines invited me up to Berlin, so I left Katharina's in Munich and headed to the capital. When I got there, Ines asked me about my future plans. I told her I wanted to continue my studies and send money to my family back home. She helped me find a university, and introduced me to Bard College in Berlin, which has a special scholarship for refugees. Bard had held a conference "Thinking Beyond Crisis" that was inspired by Hannah Arendt's philosophy; the scholarships grew out of the conference. I read Arendt's books and made comparisons between refugees in World War II and the current situation.

Bard granted me the scholarship and I was thrilled to get in. The college gave me tuition and housing, as well as a modest sum for living expenses and insurance. I was able to stop having to accept benefits offered by the German government. I started to study and was very happy! I had imagined that if I worked hard in Berlin, I would be able to get into college. But I was much luckier, because I had many people who helped me. I got my residency papers quickly and started to live in Berlin with Ines.

Once I was settled, Ines started asking me about what I would like to do: I wanted to start an Arabic-German library, something I had been thinking about. Berlin did not have any Arabic libraries. She was excited about the concept, and we began to work together. We found the perfect place: a refugee camp operated by the Red Cross, located at Stresemannstraße 95/97, Kreuzberg, Berlin. We started to ask for book donations. The Red Cross gave two full floors to Zusammenkunft, an organization that promotes intercultural exchange and backs creative projects, that let us use the space to work on our project. They valued supporting the ingenuity of a project that sought to bridge "Old Berliners and "New Berliners," who today include many refugees. Now we share this space with other people and projects. Some people lead workshops, others present music and poetry or hands-on projects for children, as well as many other activities. We have received many proposals from other organizations to showcase music, art, poetry, painting, cooking, and other cultural events. And this does not even include all the book donations we have received.

We named the library "Baynetna," which means "Between Us" in Arabic. It is a place for sharing and exchanging ideas, resources, culture, intellectual curiosity, linguistic skills, as well as being a space to connect with others. As the name suggests, it is a place to enrich one's appreciation of the experiences and cultures that are present in Berlin, where multinational people can meet and exchange their views and interests in various domains. It is much more than a simple library.

We have since moved to a new address: Breite Str. 36, 10178 Berlin. The Central Library in Berlin offered us a separate room inside their massive library, with a private entrance.

My story started in Syria, where I began a perilous journey across seven countries and two continents by boat, train, bus, car, and on foot looking for a new and peaceful life. I am so thankful to everyone who helped me on this journey and hope one day I can help others.

I also hope to one day soon have my family join me in Berlin.

Muhannad Qaiconie
(Credit: Muhannad Qaiconie)

CHAPTER 2

Those Forgotten on the Banks of Euphrates
Dima Orsho (United States)

D ima Orsho is a Syrian soprano born in Damascus. She has studied piano, clarinet, and voice at the Higher Institute of Music in Damascus, as well as at the Boston Conservatory. She has appeared as a soloist in performances throughout the Middle East, Europe, and the United States, on world-class stages such as The Opera Bastille and Théâtre de la Ville in Paris, the Bimhuis in Amsterdam, the Library of Congress in Washington, D.C., and the National Theater of Taipei. She currently composes for orchestral performances and film. In addition to her solo work, she has collaborated on several projects that address memories that she carries from her homeland.

Those Forgotten on the Banks of Euphrates: Dima Orsho (United States)

هدوة

وكل شدة على المسكين ما دامت   انتم تنامون وعين الله ما دامت
وأنتم تلمون الذهب وأني ذهب حالي   يا نايمين الليل وما حالكن حالي
وتحن عليهم يا قلبي حنين النوق عالحيران   يا نوق سيري يوم فراقهم حيران
وشكد اصبرك يا قلبي، ما تصبر بلياهم   بالليل أراهم وبالدنيا اتمناهم

Lullaby *(Hidwa)*

You sleep and the Lord watches you and all hardship on the wretched won't last

O night sleepers if only you were in my place and you harvest the gold and I harvest the pain

O camels you march, I was lost the day they left o my heart, you miss them just like camels miss their calves

I dream of them at night, and miss them in the day how much I am comforting you my heart, I know you can't live without them

The sorrow, love, and hope of a mother for her children. In 2016, I composed the lullaby's music and performed it for the first time at the Morgenland Festival in Osnabrück, Germany. These ancient lyrics, which are in the Syrian dialect spoken in the city of Deir ez-Zor, were passed down from generation to generation over centuries. I got them from a friend's grandmother who had lived in Deir ez-Zor all her life. She learned these verses from her mother, whose grandmother had passed them to her.

A mother is singing a lullaby softly and harmoniously, thus communicating it with her baby by either rocking the baby against her bosom, on her legs, or in a crib—a tradition in our culture that has roots in very ancient times. Through this tradition, there is also the mother's unique way of using her voice by rising, softening, slowing, and hastening it, depending on the child's response at the moment. In addition to the sound of the mother, the harmonious lyrics of the lullaby affect the baby. Those lyrics reflect the feelings and the wishes of a mother for the child, such as happiness, health, and getting married in the future, as well as sorrow.

Lullabies reflect the customs and traditions of our heritage. For me, they represent intimacy. They differ from one region to another, or from one culture to another, but the message is universal. Reading the translation of this lullaby, one could feel and understand the love, sorrow, grief, wishes, and hopes of a Syrian mother in Deir ez-Zor or any Syrian or non-Syrian mother. My lullaby is universal.

In Deir ez-Zor people recited poetry that expressed their daily thoughts, hopes, and longings. It took me a long time to find some authentic traditional lullabies that had been recorded. I should mention that these lullabies were not archived by educational and cultural organizations. I was able to gather several of them by contacting friends, or friends of friends, and after some time, got hold of authentic, traditional ones from Deir ez-Zor city. Of course, due to the war, it was impossible for me to go to Syria to record the lullabies.

Deir ez-Zor city, located about 450 kilometers (about 280 miles) northeast of Damascus on the banks of the Euphrates, was besieged by ISIS and the Syrian army for three years. Civilians were trapped in this region and devastated by the atrocities being committed. The city is known for its ancient trade routes including one leading from Aleppo to Baghdad, and the other from Damascus to Mosul. However, during the civil war, because of the presence of oil and gas around these cities, the route turned into a vicious war zone. Finally, in 2017, ISIS was driven out of the area.

In 2016, I composed *Those Forgotten on the Banks of the Euphrates*, a piece that sheds light upon the sorrow and suffering of the forgotten civilians in Deir ez-Zor and Raqqa cities. We heard so little about the plight of the civilians. As a Syrian-American composer and a soprano-singer, I wanted to bring awareness to what they were going through. My music and my voice were the means to tell the sad and tragic stories of those forgotten on the banks of the Euphrates. It led me to compose other works, the previously-mentioned *Hidwa (Lullaby)* and then *Ishtar: The Greater Mother*.

Music is a powerful vehicle for expressing our thoughts and emotions. The war in Syria made me think of telling the tragic stories of Syrians in order to bring awareness to their suffering. Emotions including love, hope, sorrow, grief, and pain are so intense at times that only my voice and my music have the power to express them honestly. I genuinely believe that the ability to produce music that highlights a sense of sympathy for the shattered lives of the civilians in the Syrian war is a remarkable achievement.

I was born in Damascus in 1975. My family loved art and music. My mother was a teacher, my father a computer programmer, and my brother a student. Like many other Syrian families, we were scattered due to the war. My parents live with me and my husband in the United States. My brother, who became a creative and successful architect, lives and works in Germany.

I was only seven years old when I entered Solhi Al-Wadi's music school in Damascus. In those days, it was the only music school in Syria, and was called the Arabic Institute of Music. I loved music and enjoyed performing. I participated in many musical activities and performances through the Ba'ath Vanguards organization. I enjoyed being on stage and traveling to many small towns and villages to perform. This organization had three different categories. Students in the primary school were members of the Al-Ba'ath Vanguards organization; from elementary school to high school, students were members of the Revolutionary Youth Union; and in university, students became members of the Ba'ath party. The Arab Socialist Ba'ath party had a significant influence on the educational system in Syria.

Solhi Al-Wadi was not happy about this. He wanted me to study music and practice. He advised me not to participate in these musical activities as it was all a waste of time for a serious musician, and asked me to focus on my piano lessons, and practice diligently. At first, I couldn't understand why I had to stop going to these fun venues, but then I realized that to become a professional musician I had to focus and study consistently. Upon his advice, I started to study piano with a Russian professor.

I decided to enter the Higher Institute of Music in Damascus in 1993. Solhi Al-Wadi was the director of this new Higher Institute of Music, and he wanted to start an orchestra. He told me: "We are putting together the first Syrian symphonic orchestra and we don't need any piano players now. Why don't you pick up a wind instrument?" Solhi Al-Wadi was dedicated to music and knew how to guide and support young talent. He was a firm and a demanding musician. He was determined to establish high standards in teaching music in Syria. At his suggestion, I took up the clarinet and studied at the Higher Institute of Music for five years, while simultaneously playing in the Syrian Symphonic Orchestra. The choral teacher, Professor Babenko, a talented musician and kind person, encouraged me to start singing lessons. I followed his instructions. He nurtured in me a love of singing. Singing changed my life forever.

After I received my bachelor's degree in Voice and Clarinet from the Higher Institute of Music, I attended a series of voice masterclasses in the Netherlands for a year. I was able to do this only because I had been awarded a full scholarship from the Prince Claus Fund. Afterwards, I returned to Damascus and got a lot of job offers. At first, I was thrilled: I made good money and was able to build an excellent reputation for myself. I found work writing music, singing, working in television, theater, sound recording and mixing, and playing in orchestras. It was a fabulous time for me because I had the chance to be exposed to various experiences. Then, my parents started pushing me, encouraging me to pursue graduate studies in singing. Making this move entailed an enormous amount of work, from filling out all the paperwork to recording my performances for consideration. But it paid off, as I was admitted to the Boston Conservatory the following year, where I earned a master's degree in Opera Performance. My time there added to my overall approach to music, which is culturally nuanced and brings together diverse influences, from classical music to jazz to opera and Eastern music.

In 2003, I joined the ensemble Hewar with Kinan Azmeh and Issam Rafea. We have released three albums, the most recent of which is *Letters to a Homeland*. As a solo artist, my first album was in 2008, *Arabic Lieder*, composed by Gaswan Zerikly.

In 2017, I was featured on *Sing Me Home*, an album made by Yo-Yo Ma and the Silk Road Ensemble. The recording received a Grammy Award for Best World Music. In the same year, I also collaborated with Tina Turner, Regula Curti, and other female singers from different parts of the world, performing on the recording *Awakening Beyond*. I have been fortunate to have appeared on stages in many productions all over the world.

When the popular uprising started in Syria in March 2011, I was no longer living there, but my parents were. We were all shocked by the intensity of the fighting. The destruction of cities forced migration of citizens, and the continuous factional fighting left me devastated. In 2012, my parents visited me in the U.S. and could not return to Syria due to the intensity of the Syrian war. They now live here as legal immigrants. It was never their intention to live abroad. They left everything behind.

Events at home have been so overwhelming that they have affected my work as an artist, and have led me to write many pieces and perform in major cities, on famous stages, in Europe, the Middle East, and the U.S. I will carry the torch and keep telling the stories of the voiceless and innocent civilians of Syria.

Dima Orsho
(Credit: Martina Novak)

CHAPTER 3

Berlin, I Cook with Love
Malakeh Jazmati (Germany)

M alakeh Jazmati was born in Damascus. Before the war broke out in Syria, she was studying Arabic literature and working at MTN Syria JSC, a mobile services provider. She fled Syria to Jordan, and then to Germany. In Jordan, Malakah became a television anchor and radio announcer and went on to become a successful chef in Germany.

———◆———

I am from Damascus. My family is half Christian and half Muslim. My father was a dentist and my mother, who was from Hama, graduated with a degree in English Literature. Before I left Syria, I was studying Arabic Literature and working at the MTN Syria

JSC, a mobile services provider. In March 2011, when the Syrian uprising started, I began providing financial help to families whose loved ones had been kidnapped or killed. I helped these families secretly, until the Syrian government found out and started tapping my calls.

Nobody warned me about anything. No one from the government contacted me directly, but they followed me, and my life was in danger. I went about my daily routine and continued to assist others, but this made me and everybody I came in contact with vulnerable. The government collected information about the families I was in contact with and were waiting for just the right moment to detain me.

During this time, my father was working in Saudi Arabia, and I was getting ready to travel and meet up with my family there. Before I left Syria, my father ran my personal information by the officers at the border. He was surprised to find my name on the blacklist. He realized that I would not be able to leave the country. He immediately informed me that my life was in danger and that the Syrian government could detain me at any moment. My dad paid a fortune in bribes to the customs officer at Syria's international airport; the officer hid my file and made it possible for me to pass the checkpoint and leave for Saudi Arabia. At that time, I was not aware of all these details. When I arrived in Saudi Arabia, my father told me the computer system had a double-page entry system for people on the blacklist. All Syrian citizens had one page, and those on the blacklist had a separate page. The officer my father bribed deleted my second or "blacklist" page and so I was able to leave. It sounds like a Hollywood movie, but this was my reality. It was 2012, and I was lucky to get out of Syria.

I joined my parents in Saudi Arabia, but I couldn't live there. Women were subject to rigidly defined rules, and I could not comply with those rules. I wanted to go back to Syria. My father was furious. He told me that it was impossible for me to go back to Syria. Instead, he suggested that I could go to Jordan and help the refugees in the Zaatari Refugee Camp. I started to volunteer at the camp, where daily life for refugees was appalling. My dad would send me money and donations to distribute in the refugee camp.

I became well-known among the Syrian refugee community living in Jordan and worked at the camp for a year and a half. It was a very demanding job—people needed all kinds of help including accommodations, food, water, sanitary aid, and medical care. People who once had houses and jobs now were living under tents with nothing but the clothes on their backs.

The conditions in the camp were unbearable, and after awhile, for this and other reasons, I made the decision to leave my volunteer job and start a new path. I became a television anchor and radio announcer. I spoke and wrote Arabic eloquently. My program became popular very quickly. I believe in educating Arab women, so my show focused on educational concerns in the Arab world, rather than superficial topics such as plastic surgery, a popular program topic for Arab women. Then I focused on the psychological needs of children living in war zones. My experiences in the Zaatari Refugee Camp put me in touch with so many children who were dealing with trauma. For example, I came across many children who had gone deaf over the course of the war. With proper treatment, they were able to hear again.

My cooking shows on television started also to become popular. I invited famous writers, actors, and singers to join me, and cooked with them while discussing their work. I started promoting the reading of books. I read many books and encouraged viewers to do the same, especially major Arabic books and novels. The number of readers is small compared to those in Europe or the U.S., but I was able to introduce these writers to the general public through cooking and entertainment. It was a great way to provide educational content to my audience. Beyond that, I was able to use food as a way to discuss larger issues within the Arab world. Cooking is something that varies from region to region. My guests and I could explain the way we prepared and understood our food as a way of expressing differences across cultures. I made dishes that were Syrian, though at times I would struggle to remember the recipes, and had to call my mother. At the end of each show, we would sit down and eat together.

While this was going on in Jordan, I was also a student of International Relations and Diplomacy. It was a busy time. During the day I worked at the TV station, and at night I worked at the Syrian Opposition Consulate, where I wrote all the diplomatic letters in Arabic. I stayed in Jordan for a total of three years, then left in 2015 to join my husband in Germany.

During the entire time that I was in Jordan, my husband remained in Syria. He was ultimately able to flee to Turkey, and from there, like so many others, he made the perilous sea crossing on a small dinghy. After touching ground in Europe, he made it to

Germany by train and foot, traveling from Greece to Macedonia, then through Serbia, Hungary, and Austria. He arrived in October of 2015, was recognized as a refugee and as a result, had the right to send for me since I was his wife. In 2015, 98 percent of those who arrived in Germany received refugee status; in 2018, only about 30 percent are given the full measure of protection that this status guarantees.

When I joined my husband in Germany, I left behind a successful career as an on-air chef at Orient TV, an anti-government television station that broadcast from Jordan into Syria. The first thing I did was begin studying German and English, along with trying to figure out what I could do next. I realized that cooking does not require language skills. My English and German are still very much a work in progress, but my cooking skills are part of my culture and identity. I can share my food with others and as I am doing this, I am saying: "I love you, I thank you, I miss you, I celebrate with you"—just by cooking a meal and sharing it with other people! It was in Berlin that I finally realized that I have a flair and soul for cooking. This doesn't mean that I love cooking per se, but that I love gathering with people. When a cook really loves her profession, she will innovate and create dishes that are complex and full of love. She will experiment with heat and ice to achieve certain colors, densities, textures, and taste. I started out with birthday celebrations and various other parties, and now I cook for eight hundred people!

I am like a mother who cooks to feed her children and gather her extended family and friends together to enjoy life through happy moments and events. I love what I am working towards. I bring people together, make them happy, and share my culture with the world. I let the world know that we are humans: Arabs, Syrians, and Muslims. We are well educated and live our lives similar to the ways other people in the world do. When people in Berlin eat my food, they say: "It tastes like my mother's food." And this is because my food is cooked with love, just like when a mother cooks for her family. When I first got to Berlin, I was sometimes asked to donate a simple Syrian dish or to cater a small event for a modest honorarium. After a short period of time, people spoke highly of my cooking and the news spread via word of mouth. I received a request to cater an event for 350 people, a film festival in Berlin that lasted for nine days. Accepting this request was a big risk for me: it meant my entire future—either success or failure. If I succeeded it would mean independence: I could pay taxes as a German citizen and stop receiving money from the German government. I would be able to work and pay my dues, and not just receive aid as a Syrian refugee. I took the risk, and I succeeded. Even the country's Chancellor, the most famous woman in the world, Angela Merkel, admired my cooking. Consequently, my husband and I created the Levante Gourmet, and started catering in Berlin. We have employees who handle some of the details, like handling technology issues, communicating with people, and taking orders. My husband and I work in the kitchen. We manage inventory and cook, alongside our employees.

Not long after we started our company, a publisher was interested in making a book out of my recipes. But not just my recipes—they also wanted the stories that went along with the recipes and dishes. For example, they wanted stories that explain why we eat certain foods a certain way, how the family spends hours around the table, and how each dish varies from region to region, depending on climate. In short, the meaning of our food. What does something like baba ganoush mean? Why does the best ghee come from Hama? What is the relationship between a shepherd and his herd? How is butter made from milk in the right season?

I wrote a short introduction in the book that goes like this: "I am from a country where the sun shines every day. Humans, herds, and plants live together harmoniously, and their story becomes a love story that blossoms on that heavenly land. They become artists that create attractive images of plants, turning their harvest into a labor of love. When we are in the sky, flying over the land in a plane, we see the earth laid out below us and it is painted with colors that are similar to our tables, where the hummus is next to our vegetable plates, which is next to our daily food. Our traditions of keeping our harvest healthy with our sweat, love of labor, and hard work reflects the sweat, love of labor, and hard work that characterizes our cuisine. That is why our vegetables are delicious and our cooked meals are mouthwatering. We do it all with love. When you walk into a vegetable market and try our vegetables, the smell and taste are out of this world! You feel like you are eating the bounty of paradise. All you have to do is visit a farm that has cows and taste a glass of milk. You will sample the distinct flavor of the sugar cane fields that cows have grazed on, the time it ripened, and when the milk was produced. Our food reflects our seasons. During times when it is hot, we eat vegetables that keep us cool, and when it is cold we eat vegetables that give us energy and keep us warm. In my country, food is a way to connect with our family, neighbors, and society at large. This is especially true with foods that are expensive, for we know how to share with the poor and the needy living in the streets."

As far as I am concerned, Syrian cuisine represents our civilization. I wanted to share our history, culture, and enlightenment through my cookbook. The book was initially in German, then translated into Dutch, and soon will be available in French and English.

I love Syria, my country, and I hope this war will end soon. The question is, though, will we go back? I have two answers to this question. One, if war ceases and Syria needs helping hands, those of us living in the diaspora must help rebuild the country. If not, it could be like Iraq, where the natives did not return, and chaos replaced everything. However, on the other hand, Germany gave us a chance to start a new life, and we, as new citizens of Germany, should give back to the country we owe so much to—the country that saved us. I have a son, and I must think about his life as much as my husband's and my own.

My dream is to be with my extended family. My father died a year after I arrived in Jordan. My mother is now in Jordan, and I haven't seen her since I left Saudi Arabia. Nowadays, it is hard to bring your parents into Germany unless you can sponsor them. My husband and I are working very hard, and we hope one day my mother will join us.

Malakeh Jazmati
(Credit: Malakeh Jazmati)

CHAPTER 4

The Kiss to the World
Tammam Azzam (Germany)

Tammam Azzam was born in Damascus. He graduated from the Faculty of Fine Arts at the University of Damascus, where he majored in oil painting. Tammam was a prolific artist in Syria and had a successful career as a painter and graphic designer. In 2011 he relocated to Dubai, and he has had many international exhibitions including at Bienal del Sur, Caracas; Künstlerforum Bonn, Bonn; FOR-SITE Foundation, San Francisco; European Capital of Culture-Pafos, Pafos, Cyprus; City Museum of Oldenburg, Oldenburg, Germany; Künstlerverein Walkmühle, Wiesbaden, Germany; Columbia University, New York; Tainiothiki Twixtlab, Athens; Ayyam Gallery – 11 Alserkal Avenue, Dubai; Banksy's Dismaland, Weston-super-Mare in

Somerset, England; Fondazione Giorgio Cini, Venice; Framer Framed in de Tolhuistuin, Amsterdam; Forum Factory, Berlin; Lena & Roselli Gallery, Budapest; Liquid Art House, Boston; Rush Arts, New York; Busan Museum of Art, Seoul; and 1x1 Art Gallery, New Delhi. In 2016, Azzam received an artist fellowship at the Hanse-Wissenschaftskolleg Institute for Advanced Study in Delmenhorst, Germany. Azzam resides in Germany with his wife and daughter. He did not apply for refugee status to live in Germany.

———◆———

I left Damascus with my wife and daughter for Dubai in 2011, just after the beginning of the revolution that grew into a massive, multisided armed conflict, driving millions of Syrians from Syria. To many Syrians, living in the country became a nightmare of being hunted down, besieged, imprisoned, or killed. The pulsations of love, the pain of defeat, the exhilaration of resistance, the falling and then standing up—again and again—was a struggle that had no end.

In Syria, my works were in a hybrid form of painting with oil and various media that made me able to create physical interactions between surface and form. These works included ropes, clothespins, and other found objects so that I could intensify the depth, texture, and space of pictures' planes, generating a visible tension. My themes were about the changing perceptions of specific urban environments.

In 2013, my art took the world by storm. I was living in Dubai with my family, lacking studio space and art supplies, when I turned to digital media and graphic art. Although I was living safely with my family in Dubai, mentally I was still in Damascus. I felt a more significant need to express my thoughts and my sadness, and to respond to what was happening in Syria. I wanted to draw a parallel between the most magnificent creations of—and horrific destruction caused by—humans. I digitally superimposed Gustav Klimt's *The Kiss* on a photograph of a bombed-out building in an unknown part of Syria. Klimt's *The Kiss* portrays the love and relationship between humans; I juxtaposed this with the hate the regime has for its citizens, and the destruction it has caused.

This image, known as "The Freedom Graffiti," went viral, with more than two hundred thousand people sharing it on social media since London's Saatchi Gallery shared it. I wanted to tell stories about Syrian people, myself, and people everywhere on this planet. My theme was universal, and not only for Syrians. I consider my artwork timeless and as universally relatable today as it was in the past, and will be in future. With all modesty, I do not compare myself with Picasso, but I could say the same about Picasso's *Guernica*, which was a visual response to the brutal massacre of civilians in a small town in Spain. *Guernica* is primarily a war painting, showing a visual account of the devastating and chaotic impact of war on people, and especially on civilian life and communities, but at the same time, it expresses a universal theme of brutality and death of defenseless civilians.

Although having worked with different media over the last several years, my creations shed light on the same urgent theme: the ongoing political and social turmoil in Syria, and the continuous waves of violence causing destruction and migration of Syrians. My latest works of art (*Paper Series*) are developed towards abstraction, as is the Syrian war—becoming distant to the rest of the world while defenseless civilians back home live in one of the bloodiest conflicts in the world today. Through the use of collage and bright, lively colors, I am rebuilding my country and society and calling for a peaceful reminder of Syria's civil war. Empathy should not be only for the new world.

Tammam Azzam
(Credit: Khaled Youssef)

CHAPTER 5

Feeling Like Home
Mojahed Akil (Turkey)

M ojahed Akil is from Aleppo, Syria, where he studied computing as a university student. After fleeing Syria in 2013 and settling in Turkey, he adapted his skills to serve the needs of the rapidly expanding migrant population by creating a website and app called *Gherbtna*, which means "exile," "loneliness," or "foreignness" in Arabic. The app provides much needed guidance in the confusing and disorienting process of establishing a new home in Turkey. The site has reached millions of users and has received many awards, including recognition from Google. Akil hopes to bring his professional knowledge back to Syria one day when the country is ready to rebuild. He currently resides in Istanbul, Turkey.

Feeling Like Home: Mojahed Akil (Turkey)

———◆•◆———

After being detained by the Syrian regime forces, I decided to leave the country on September 25, 2013. I did not have time to pack, so I only brought a few items of clothing and my laptop. I left Aleppo, crossed the border and ended up in Kilis, a town in the south of Turkey. I stayed there for a few days, and then continued to Gaziantep.

Before I left Syria, I had studied computer engineering and had my own business providing technology services; I knew how to design websites and create software to fit a client's specifications. Even though these skills are very transferable, my most significant barrier in Turkey was not being able to speak the language. Having skills and talent but not being able to communicate with the natives made my life very difficult. I could not complete even the most basic paperwork, buy food, find housing or a job, or navigate the city. People in Gaziantep could not speak English, French, or Arabic. I was not the only Syrian forced migrant who was facing these challenges. Millions of Syrians had fled, and settling into this new country was hard for all of us.

I was able to work from home as a freelancer for six months, and then joined a technology company that specialized in web design and development. My salary was decent, and soon the company started offering me Turkish language lessons. I became fluent within a short time and decided to create a website and application called Gherbtna to help the Syrian community adjust to life in Turkey.

I launched this project with another person and, after working on it for eight months, we developed a fully functional website and application. It offers a variety of support, but the overall aim is to help migrants figure out the confusing process of settling in Turkey. For example, there are sections that deal with job openings, university registration instructions, residency permit laws, opening bank accounts, completing medical papers, and more. There is also up-to-date information on the state of affairs at the border, such as the status of shelling, and safe points of passage. Perhaps most importantly, it also provides a link to a live translator who can communicate with people in Turkish!

Another essential part of the project is that it provides information on the Syrian community, at home and abroad. I remember very well that when I first arrived in Turkey, there was not any news broadcast about Syrians still in Syria. With this application, a person can listen to the news in Arabic about what is going on both in Turkey and at home. A person can look for an answer to almost any concern just by surfing on this one site. Thus, anyone who suffers from lack of information could use the app to find solutions to daily challenges. Both the website and application became popular with the Syrian community living in Turkey. Initially, we designed it for Android handsets, but then it became available for download on other smartphones, such as the iPhone and Windows Phone.

The name we chose for the app, Gherbtna, is an Arabic word that has a combined meaning of loneliness, exile, and living away from one's homeland. It is a concept that resonates very well with the millions of Syrians who became displaced and ended up in Turkey. So many Syrians have had to leave their homes, families, and jobs, take refuge in foreign lands, and start new lives. Every day I share the sufferings and hardships of Syrian refugees. We have all had to leave behind everything, even our families, and start over. Everyone has had to struggle every day to stay alive and put bread on the table. Everyone is seeking a better life. I started to think about how I could reach these people and make their lives easier. And that's where the idea came from: I could provide useful information about the country that we were all once living in happily (Syria), and the country we now call home (Turkey).

In the beginning, I offered these services for free, but then Syrian companies started to advertise on the website. Restaurants, trading companies, wedding reception halls, and many other professionals noticed our application and wanted to place ads and announcements. We started to receive income, and we grew exponentially. Now I have a big company with many employees.

In 2016, Google invited me to San Francisco to present my application at the annual Google I/O 2016 App Developers meeting. Unfortunately, I couldn't get an American visa. Instead, Google created a video about the services we offered and presented it to the seven thousand attendees at the annual Google I/O 2016 Conference. It was shown live on the internet. This type of exposure opened new doors for me. For example, a Turkish technology company has expressed interest in working with us.

We also founded two Arabic magazines called *Gherbtna*, a social, educational, and commercial magazine, and *Gherbtna Training*, a publication dedicated to training and developing technology skills, web design, and teaching of the Turkish language. Both magazines are available in Mersine, Gaziantep, and Istanbul cities.

I was able to educate and help many Syrians who are now able to work in Turkey, and some already have joined my company. I miss my homeland, Syria, and hope one day I can return and help rebuild my country.

Mojahed Akil
(Credit: Mojahed Akil)

CHAPTER 6

The Power of Music
Kinan Azmeh (United States)

Kinan Azmeh was born in Damascus, and he studied music at both the Higher Institute of Music in Damascus and the Juilliard School of Music in New York. An acclaimed composer and clarinetist, he was described as "engagingly flamboyant" by the *Los Angeles Times* and hailed as a "virtuoso" and "intensely soulful" by *The New York Times*. In addition to his solo work, Kinan has collaborated with many outstanding artists from both Eastern and Western traditions, including the ensemble *Hewar*; Yo-Yo Ma's *Silk Road Ensemble*; and pianist Dinuk Wijeratne. He has performed at some of the world's most prestigious venues, including the Opera Bastille in Paris and Carnegie Hall in New York. He is a member of Yo-Yo Ma's Silk Road Ensemble, and with whom he was awarded a Grammy in 2017. He spends much of his time touring and collaborating but calls New York City his home.

⟶•⟶

I know that music won't stop a bullet or feed the hungry, but it can bring empathy and joy to the world.

I was born and grew up in Damascus, and started playing clarinet at the Arab Conservatory of Music. I kept up my musical studies at the Higher Institute of Music in Damascus, even as I was concurrently receiving a bachelor's degree in electrical engineering at the University of Damascus. After winning the Nikolai Rubinstein International Youth Competition Award in Moscow in 1997, I decided to head to the U.S. and attend Juilliard, just one week before the September 11, 2001 attacks on the United States. Being an Arab was not easy because of all the new immigration rules that were put into place after the attacks. I was continuously considered a suspect just because I held a Syrian passport. Even so, in addition to completing my studies at Julliard, I also received a doctorate in music from the City University of New York.

Since completing my studies, I have traveled the world a lot, both as a soloist and composer, as well as a member of orchestras and chamber ensembles. I have organized live music performances that involve film, animated illustrations, and electronic art (involving technology that is used to project painting and music simultaneously). I am in the spotlight 95 percent of the time I'm performing. I love being on stage—I'm a person who enjoys sharing my secrets with people. Being on stage is like being on the top of the mountain, feeling free to reveal all my secrets. There is something very empowering about being on stage and sharing my thoughts and feelings.

Outside of music, I love being in nature, working with the dirt and soil: making holes, planting trees, running in the rain. I love being in the rain. It reminds me of being in Syria! I'm never alone or entirely "off stage": my family, friends, Damascus, and New York City are all in my thoughts when I am composing. I am never alone. I meet a lot of new people. I love writing music and enjoy performing my pieces. I have multiple concerts throughout the year. Sometimes my wife joins me on tour, and sometimes I join her (she is also a touring musician). When I am not touring, I have my daily rituals. I start my day with exercise, either by going to Brighton Beach to swim or riding my bicycle. I then work on my compositions, meet friends, and make new acquaintances. But I love performing and traveling the world throughout the year.

People often ask me when I tour the U.S. if I think the public understands what I am saying in my music. This question doesn't concern me very much. The best thing about making art is that it is open to a gazillion possibilities. Every time you play a musical phrase, it is exciting to know that the connection between the senses and the brain of the recipient is how they experience that music. If I were able to summarize in words or speech what I want to say through my music, I would. It would be easier. But, since music is the most abstract form of art one can hear and interpret, it produces different meanings and thoughts. It makes me happy that what I'm presenting to my listeners is not monochrome.

The Power of Music: Kinan Azmeh (United States)

Everything is open to different interpretations. For me, music has to do with experiencing emotions that I have not experienced before. A sad song is not just a sad song; similarly, a happy song is not just a happy one. That's too simple. What we respond to when listening to a piece of music is how it moves us. I don't think that language has the capacity of explaining what happens to us. This feeling differs from one person to another and has a different impact on each of us. It is an intimate emotion. I don't think audiences are actually all that different. People often like to separate the audiences of the Middle East, Europe, and the United States, but for me, they blend together: I don't know where one starts and the other ends. Art should have three things, and this is what audiences expect: First, they want to see somebody who has something to say. Second, the artist must have a tool through which he can communicate the message. Third, the artist must possess the skill, passion, and dedication to communicate with the tools he has. Members of the audience are aware when this takes place. Everyone enjoys it when they see musicians relishing their time on stage. When a performance works well, even if you don't have a trained ear, you will still enjoy that performance.

The problem I find with people is that when they listen to you and are not familiar with where you are from geographically, they want to categorize you. I don't like to classify people by breaking them into herds by saying: "This is African music, this is European music," and so on. People try to categorize my music as Arabic. It's not, and that's the problem. But it's not *my* problem. I am here to educate people through my music and make them curious enough to check out other stuff that lies beyond their comfort zone. In

Europe you might enjoy Bach, Mozart, or a gypsy clarinetist from Hungary, or Syrian or Lebanese songs, and so on. These categories do not concern me much. That's how I listen to music, especially when friends give me CDs and ask me to listen to their music. The most important thing is to keep discovering new ideas and thoughts. The best thing you can do as an artist or a human being is to remain curious and not fall into a comfort zone, in whatever you do.

Even if my audience does not have an understanding of Oriental modes and scales, I think they can understand me. If you listen to the last movement of Beethoven's *Ninth Symphony*, something which even schoolchildren can hum, can you summarize what Beethoven wanted in writing? Nobody can do that. It is one of the most famous classical music pieces in the Western tradition. Learning from music is not about summarizing what the composer wants to say. There is a word we sometimes forget in these conversations: pleasure. There is an important question anyone can ask me: "Kinan, why do you do what you do?" My answer? Pleasure.

I don't believe that you necessarily must understand something academically to receive pleasure from it. When I go on stage to perform, the experience gives me great pleasure in the same way a concert provides the listener with great enjoyment. People go to performances for different reasons, and they all listen to a variety of music genres. If someone has listened to Oriental music all his life and one day hears Schubert, Schumann, and Beethoven, he may tell you it all sounds the same. This person may not get it and say that what he is listening to sounds monotone. The same thing could be said about any other kind of music if one has not been exposed to it. It is true for any art form that stimulates the brain.

When I compose music, my background is always part of what I create. Today, Syria is suffering from unrest and Syrians both inside and outside of the country are suffering. But whether that influences what I write depends. It has a lot to do with why I do what I do. Sometimes I write music in reaction to something that has happened. And sometimes I want to write music to escape from something. I have always felt that I'm somebody who is both politically and humanly aware of what is happening in this world. Syria is home to me, so of course it is my most influential platform. There is lots of Syria in my music compositions. What I do is not traditional, that's for sure. But what I do is undoubtedly inspired by planting a tree in Damascus, or walking in the rain with my friends, or playing soccer on the concrete with my friends and breaking my bones, or playing at the schoolyard with my friends. Those are *my* stories from *my* childhood memories of Syria. These memories indeed shape who I am.

I try to be socially engaged now with what I do now, especially throughout the last six years, because I believe I have a powerful tool in my hand that I must use. If Syria and its people are not in the news, that does not mean that the civil unrest has stopped, or the forced migrations have disappeared. The tragedy continues. I have the luxury of having an instrument that can express my vision, through my compositions and performances. I am also like any other human being, living in a world with so many issues. Human beings are destroying pretty much everything we have on this planet. We all face environmental and global humanitarian problems every day. The human brain can absorb a certain amount of tragedy, but we owe it to ourselves to celebrate the life we have. So sometimes I write music and express joy and everything that is fantastic in life. I don't only think of the tragedies—I celebrate joy and happiness as well.

I encourage people to move away from the continuum that questions what is classical or not. I want to break the barrier that exists between East and West. People should think outside the box, take risks, and get out of their comfort zones. Orchestras and concert halls should also think outside the box since there is so much magnificent music that should be performed and enjoyed.

I want to go and see musicians taking risks and reaching out to audiences. Having music from the Arab world in New York or anywhere in the world should not be considered exotic. It should be a natural fabric of what this country has, given the diverse population living in it. The less categorization we do, the better we are as world citizens.

My hope is that Syria becomes a free and democratic secular country. I hope for a lot of other things to happen, but if I attempt to talk about all of them, this conversation would never end. I want to continue composing and performing music, and hope I can continue to be excited about what I do.

Kinan Azmeh
(Credit: Martina Novak)

CHAPTER 7

The Compassionate Teacher
Lena Tavitian (Canada)

*L*ena Tavitian was born in Beirut. After graduating from high school, she left for Yerevan, Armenia, studied Armenian language and literature, and received her master's from Yerevan State University. She has been teaching Armenian language and literature since 1986.

Lena is my second cousin. We grew up together and attended the Yervant Demirdjian School in Beirut (1967-1974). She lived through the Lebanese Civil War and left Syria for Canada before the current war began, but has stayed connected with many Syrian civilians.

The Compassionate Teacher: Lena Tavitian (Canada)

When I think of great teachers, of course I think of my professors who have personally changed my life, such as Rafael Ishkhanyan, a linguist, philologist, and historian, and Pavel Sharabkhanyan, a brilliant linguist who taught me Classical Armenian language. I should mention that when I studied in Armenia, we used to call our professors "Comrade" instead of using the title "Professor." At that time Armenia was part of the U.S.S.R., and the education system in Armenia followed the rules and criteria of the Soviet educational system. Both of my professors were genuinely passionate and excited about what they taught, and that joy of pursuing knowledge inspired me.

I left Lebanon in 1980 for Yerevan to pursue my higher education in Armenian language and literature. My years living and studying in Yerevan had an enormous impact on my life. I truly valued my university environment: to me, it was a haven where I was respected, valued, and able to relax, all of which enabled me to learn and socialize. Every day, my professors demonstrated their passion, dedication, knowledge, and personal engagement to their teaching. Their inspiration was contagious; attending lectures where they spoke passionately and expertly on a subject lit a fire within me, and made me want to learn and dive more in-depth in my courses.

I graduated in 1986 with a master's degree in Armenian Language and Literature and returned to Beirut. I taught Armenian language and literature at Boghos K. Garmirian School until 1990.

During this time (from 1988 to 1990), Lebanon experienced the intra-Christian war. Life was difficult due to daily bombings. It took me ten minutes to commute to the school from my home in Rabyah, an upscale suburban area in the northern part of greater Beirut. Whenever the shelling started, we left the school at once and I was able to return home within a few minutes. I loved working with young students and sharing my knowledge and passion for teaching Armenian language and culture. The civil war in Beirut created a lot of anxiety between students and parents. As a teacher, personal engagement with students was an essential element in teaching, followed by the sharing of knowledge. As a teacher, I had to engage with my students and create a safe environment at a time when the country was caught up in a civil war. There were days we had peaceful classes, and students were able to go outside for recreation. On other days, we had to stay in the building or leave the school at once.

Living in Beirut was tough due to the civil war. I wanted to keep my connections with my classmates from Yerevan State University. The phones did not work correctly, the mail system was corrupt, the electricity went on and off, and water supplies were limited. I felt isolated from the world. The only way I could get letters from bordering countries was through taxi drivers. My university boyfriend lived in Syria—he kept in contact with me during all these years, and we decided to get married in 1990. He studied Civil Engineering and worked in Aleppo, Syria. It was a relief for me to leave Lebanon during the civil war, but at the same time, it was hard to leave behind my family, friends, and students. Upon my arrival at Aleppo, the AGBU Lazar Najarian-Calouste Gulbenkian

School offered me a teaching position. Over sixteen years, I taught hundreds of students. It was a joyful experience to work with young minds, teach Armenian language and culture, and share my expertise in this environment. Both students and parents loved me, and I was often invited to their houses and asked to participate in other venues.

During this time, I had two children, both boys. My husband and I had to think ahead and make decisions for them. Syria had a compulsory military service, which meant both my sons would have to serve in the military. The region (the Middle East) was a volatile place. I had lived through the civil war in Lebanon; many young men—both Lebanese and Syrian—died without purpose. We decided to migrate to Canada and build a new life with our children. Once again, it was a heartbreaking decision to leave behind all our relatives, friends, colleagues, and students and start a new life in a new country.

In 2006 we arrived in Montreal as legal immigrants. At that time, there was no war in Syria. In Montreal, our first difficulty was the language. We were all educated in English but did not know French. My children were distraught that we uprooted them and brought them to Canada. They did not have any friends. We had to learn where the market and hospital were, and how to drive in this new land. Both of my children suffered from loneliness and sometimes were bullied at school because they were different than the locals. The fierce winter weather was horrendous. Living in the Middle East, the weather was mild and sunny most of the time. We did not have the proper clothes in Canada to keep us warm. In addition, we had to find occupations and a place to live. It took us two years to settle down and find our bearings in Montreal.

I started to teach at Armen-Quebec Alex Manoogian School. Besides teaching Armenian language and literature, I had to integrate the Armenian culture in my other classes. I had to create many celebrations in Armenian. Students had to sing, recite, and act. In 2011 the Syrian war started, and the Hay Doun in Montreal decided to bring Syrian refugees to Canada. Hay Doun, which means "Armenian Home," offers family support services to refugees and provides social education and integration into the community. It has many volunteers yet few employees. I started to get many phone calls from Aleppo: relatives, neighbors, and parents of my Syrian students. They all heard of this opportunity to come to Canada and needed sponsorship and guidance. My husband and I started to visit Hay Doun and learn about their requirements. Like us, every Armenian in Canada had a loved one in Syria, and they wanted to help them. Syrian refugees had to go to Beirut—once their papers were organized and they were sponsored by a Canadian family, hundreds of Syrian families started to land in Montreal. Every day at school I got calls from Syrian people reaching out to me, asking me how I could help them. Being a teacher in Syria for many years, I had a great wide reach and influence. I started to notice that some of my students had grown up, married, had families, and needed help. I reached out to my neighbors and friends in Canada to help these refugees. I had already sponsored two families and couldn't sponsor more, but I was able to connect with parents at my school and ask each family to help the Syrian refugees. I visited Hay Doun; gathered coats, kitchen utensils, and boots; and donated them. Many other people did the same.

One day when I arrived at Hay Doun, the snow was up to my knees. I was still in my car and saw an elderly woman and her daughter exiting the bus and walking towards Hay Doun. It reminded me of when our family did not have a car and had to use public transportation during fiercely cold weather. I felt sorry for the old woman, and followed them to Hay Doun. They met with one of the employees and came out with a big box. I asked the elderly woman what was in the box, and if she was planning on carrying it to her house. I was shocked when she told me that it was a computer, and that she had to take the bus again with her daughter to return home. I immediately offered them a ride in my car and took both to their house. They were strangers and needed help. Both were so thankful and invited me to have a coffee in their house. I did not stay and returned to my own home. This was not the first time such things happened. People in the supermarket have approached me and asked, "Are you Mrs. Lena?" Most of the time, they were former students of mine from Syria. They hugged me. I asked them if they needed any help or support.

My sons are studying statistics and pharmacy, and would like to return to Syria one day and see their childhood school, town, and the city of Aleppo. Our family, like many Syrian families, is scattered all over the world. I have a brother-in-law in Armenia and another in Canada; my sister-in-law is in the United States, and my mother-in-law is also in Canada. Every Syrian family has a similar story.

We as a community in Montreal help any Syrian refugees who approach us. As I write this, we are expecting a Syrian family to land in Montreal. We have sponsored them to come here. Being a compassionate teacher in Lebanon and Syria helped me assist many Syrian refugee families. Many have contacted me, and I have supported them selflessly. I thank my professors who encouraged me, and taught me how to be a passionate, as well as compassionate, teacher and person. I will keep on supporting Syrian refugee families.

Lena Tavitian
(Credit: Armen Alemian)

CHAPTER 8

Syrian Voices Echo in the World
Talar Dekrmanjian (The Netherlands)

T alar Dekrmanjian was born in Aleppo and developed a love for singing at an early age. She studied composition and voice in Damascus, Amsterdam, and Paris. She has had many significant achievements in her operatic career, including performances throughout Europe and the Middle East. Talar's roles have included Frasquita *(Carmen)*, Lauretta *(Gianni Schicchi)*, Elisetta *(Il matrimonio segreto)*, Calypso *(Ulisse)*, Micaëla *(Carmen)*, Fiordiligi *(Così fan tutte)*, and the lead in *Cendrillon*. She has also performed as a solo artist in Paris, New York, Tokyo, Moscow, and Genoa. Talar received the prize for the most distinguished artist at the Bellini Competition in Italy in 1999, and was a finalist in the Queen Elisabeth Competition in 2004. She currently resides in Brussels, Belgium.

———•◦•———

When I was in the sixth grade at Saint Thérèse School, an Armenian Catholic school in Aleppo, Soeur Anaïs, one of the school's nuns, discovered my voice. One day, as I was singing along with the choir, she approached me, hesitated, and became transfixed. She asked me to step aside and sing unaccompanied. As I finished doing what she asked of me, I noticed that my performance moved her deeply. She immediately whisked me away and brought me to the principal's office. She then introduced me to all the sisters in the school and boasted that she had discovered a promising young talent—the other nuns had faith in her judgment. Immediately, a call went home to my mother, urging her to recognize my gift and support it with professional singing lessons. My mother had no idea: I was a shy girl and did not enjoy drawing attention to myself, so both of us were surprised by this newly found celebrity.

My mother, a lifelong painter, was ecstatic. Both she and my father were great lovers of art. She could not wait to support me and find a professional mentor in Aleppo. She was willing to sacrifice all she had so that I could receive top-notch, professional voice lessons. In fact, the experience held a familiar poignancy for her—she too had attended St. Thérèse where a sister at the school recognized her gift for painting. However, my grandmother did not support her talent. In fact, she flat out forbade my mother to paint, so my mother was only able to do it surreptitiously. She tried to

81

sneak in painting sessions at home, but if my grandmother caught a whiff of paint, she not only took away her materials, but humiliated and denigrated my mother.

My grandmother was a victim of the prevailing morality of the time, which meant painting was a shameful pursuit for girls. This devastated my mother. More than anything, she wanted to take professional painting lessons, but this was out of the question. She found solace at school with the nuns. One kind sister promised to get her the supplies she needed as long as my mother paid for them. And this was all she needed. At once, she began handing over all of her pocket money for supplies and the opportunity to paint while at school. So, when my mother received a call from the very same school that day, she was determined not to repeat the same mistake. She immediately began looking for the best classical singing teacher she could afford. Back then, there was no professional opera in Syria. But she tracked down someone who turned out to be an ideal mentor, Arax Chekijian, a protégé of the Armenian opera singer Datevig Sazantarian.

After meeting me, Arax Chekijian told my mother that, with hard work and lessons, I could become an opera singer. No one in my family had any clue about opera. Opera was nonexistent in Syria, and European-style classical singing was similarly unfamiliar. We trusted in Ms. Chekijian, who insisted that I take classes with her once I turned eighteen. At first, I took lessons twice a week. I started to participate in school functions and social celebrations held by the Armenian community in Aleppo. I began to sing selections from *Anoush*, an Armenian opera.

The time finally came for me to enroll in the Higher Institute of Music in Damascus. Ms. Chekijian had prepared me well for the entrance exam. During my audition, Mr. Solhi Al-Wadi, the highly regarded director of the school, asked me: "Are you a graduate of Armenia now seeking entrance to our school here in Damascus?" to which I replied, "No, I am from Aleppo. I studied with Ms. Chekijian, and now I would like to attend the Higher Institute of Music in Damascus." I was the only student in the entire conservatory who had any training and yet, I had never heard any classical music in my life. The only music I knew came from Armenian opera.

Throughout my training, I tried to mimic Arax's way of singing. I idolized her and wanted to sing just as she did. At that time in Syria, there was only one place where I could obtain any access to classical music: a little shop that sold classical music on cassettes. There was no YouTube, no internet, no iTunes! I could not get my hands on sheet music. Solhi Al-Wadi had to place special orders for that sort of thing, and we had to wait weeks to get it. Now, of course, it's easy!

By that time, I realized how much I loved singing—it was my passion, and I knew that it was what I wanted to do with the rest of my life. I began studying at the Higher Institute of Music as a soprano lyric. I worked with a Russian instructor, and for the first three years, I made the five-hour commute between Damascus and Aleppo to continue working with Ms. Chekijian. I loved and cherished my original teacher's technique and was wary of my new teacher's instruction.

During these crazy years of commuting between Damascus and Aleppo, I kept permanent residence at a convent in Damascus. The convent had a strict curfew of 8 p.m., so I soon moved to another convent that provided me an extra hour: it closed at 9 p.m. While I was at this second convent, I would have to have Solhi Al-Wadi write the sisters a letter every time I had a performance, as I would inevitably miss my curfew. This soon became unsustainable, so I left the convent and rented a room from a family in Damascus. I lived in Damascus for seven years—five as a student, then two as a soloist with the Syrian Orchestra. After graduation, Solhi al-Wadi took me to the Consulate of the Netherlands, seeking an opportunity for me to study in Maastricht. He did all of the paperwork for me, and I got accepted to study there for three years. I was at the Zuyd Hogeschool for three years, from 2001 to 2004, and was awarded a master's degree in music with distinction. During my time there, the professors at the conservatory encouraged me to enter the Queen Elisabeth Competition, an international contest in Belgium. I competed and became one of the finalists.

The Queen Elisabeth Competition changed my entire life. Because of it, I met José van Dam, and new doors began to open for me. José was part of the finalists' judging panel, which had to consider six or seven contestants that had been narrowed down from hundreds of competitors. I met him during the semifinalist stage, and he offered me a place at Queen Elisabeth Chapel in Brussels, Belgium. I accepted his offer, moved to Belgium, and studied with him for another three years. Under him, I went through the cycle de perfectionnement, a course of study intended to polish my performance and style. Then, from 2007 to 2009, I lived in

Paris where I studied at École Normale de Musique de Paris Alfred Cortot and received a Diplome Superieur de Consertiste. I started to have many opportunities to perform.

I feel that destiny has led me down this path in life; one thing has always led to the next. Solhi al-Wadi helped me to get to Holland, then my conservatory in Holland selected me to participate in the Queen Elisabeth Competition. From there, I became one of the finalists and was offered classes with José van Dam, which took me to Belgium. Everything fell into my lap, but I also worked hard, and took things very seriously. My home became Belgium. I guess I can say that I've "made it." I am an opera singer.

Back in 1997, when I was a second-year student at the conservatory in Damascus, Zaid Jabri, a Syrian composer, won first prize for his *Two Songs for Soprano and String Orchestra* compositions at the Adam Didur Composers' Competition in Sanok, Poland. Solhi Al-Wadi asked me to perform the work in Damascus. The two pieces were contemporary songs, and presenting them was a fantastic experience for me. I did well, and the performance was a great hit! Solhi Al-Wadi was so proud of me, and so happy to have these songs performed in Damascus. Zaid was also delighted, and soon enough, he became recognized the world over as a composer. He continued to win other prestigious awards; his pieces became well-known and many artists started to perform them. We lost touch over time, and for years, I did not even know where he was. Finally, in 2015, he contacted me when he saw my performances in Europe and Russia on YouTube. He told me he was composing a new opera and the jury panel had selected me to perform his composition at Covent Garden in London. He was very firm with me, saying: "I did not choose you. The casting panel chose you, and I would be honored to have you sing my composition at the Royal Opera House as Wadha (Cities of Salt) in the Linbury Studio Theatre, London."

I was thrilled! The conductor, the stage manager, and the selection panel had chosen me to perform. The opera, called *Cities of Salt*, had three acts with a full orchestra, twelve soloists, and a chorus.

I did everything I could to prepare well and was ecstatic see my name on the Royal Opera House's website. I was humbled and honored to have the chance to sing Zaid's work in London. What a life!

In 2012, Maria João Pires took over the piano department at Queen Elisabeth Chapel Music. She wanted to create socially-minded projects and thus started a chorus of underprivileged children. Maria heard me performing and admired my singing. After a few years, she asked me to join her project. I had never had any experience in training children's voices, but I accepted her offer and worked with the children's choir. I have to say, it was incredible to see how fabulously these kids sang. At first, most of them were aggressive and showed signs of being traumatized. But with time, they calmed down, and we started to get to work. My husband is an accomplished pianist, and together, we threw ourselves into the project and tried to help the children. After two years of work, these kids performed beautifully. Now, as head of the chorus department, as well as voice coach, I organize concerts and performances. This experience has brought a different kind of satisfaction to me—one that I cannot get from my solo performances. Maria João Pires believed in giving back to the society, and so do I. The fact is, it's not enough to perform and *not* help others. I have been surprised at how I have been able to find the time to do this, and how much satisfaction this work has brought me.

Until 2011, I went to Syria every summer. I would see my friends in Aleppo, where I grew up, and I would also find my way to Damascus, where I lived and studied as a young adult. In 2010, my dad died, a life-changing event for me. It's difficult for me to speak about him even now. His death came out of nowhere: he had pancreatic cancer, and within a few months he was gone. My parents were rooted in Syria. Even though they had passports, they never thought of leaving, though my dad did visit the U.S. frequently. When his cancer spread, he had stomach pains and went to the best hospitals in the U.S. for help, but no one could help him. In the end, I left everything I was doing and stayed with him for his final months in the U.S., where he died. He was buried in Aleppo. It was a tough time for me. I was always sad, and it was very hard to sing.

In 2011, before the civil war started in Syria, the Damascus Opera House invited me to play the role of Lauretta, the female lead in Puccini's *Gianni Schicchi*. The Italian singers who took the rest of the parts traveled from Italy to Syria to perform with me. It was an honor. I was the only Syrian performer, and I had the lead role! Then, with time, some of the smaller parts were given to Syrian singers. At the time, Damascus had its first opera venue, and it was exciting. But unfortunately, after this work's run was over, the war started in Syria.

That same year, as the civil war started, my mom and brother were in Aleppo. The two of them had taken over my father's business after his death. He had a large furniture store. One day, my brother received a phone call from a terrorist group. The caller said that he wanted three million Syrian lire in cash, due the following day. My brother ignored it. Two days later, a call came in again, this time asking for fifteen million Syrian lire. And this time, the caller said that if my brother didn't pay, they would kill either my brother or mother. At this point, my mother was in mourning and therefore did not go to the store every day, so my brother had an employee helping him in the gallery. Instantly, my brother and mother became very afraid. They secretly left their house and hid in my maternal aunt's house. They knew they were being followed, and it was clear to them that their followers knew that my father was dead. The two of them hid out for fifteen days, and while they were at my aunt's, my sister and her husband went by their house to get some things for them. But when they got to the house, they saw militias with walkie-talkies standing at the entrance and were too scared to go in. They couldn't get anything out of the house. And since they knew they were being followed, they couldn't do anything—they were paralyzed. On another day, my sister and her husband were able to sneak into the house and pack up two suitcases' worth of things. She felt like a thief inside her own home. After that, my family closed up the furniture shop and the family house, and my brother and mom fled Syria. It was 2011, and they haven't returned since. They needed cash, but were only able to sell one of their two cars and withdraw a small amount of cash from the bank before leaving for the U.S.

When my mother and brother arrived in the U.S., they only had two pieces of luggage and some cash. On their way over, they stopped in Belgium, and we were able to spend some time together. Shortly after their departure, my sister left Syria too. At first, she just went with her kids to visit my mother, but then things got worse and her husband, a doctor, realized that he had to leave too. Now everyone is together in the U.S. My mother bought my sister's plane ticket for her visit. For the first month and a half, they stayed with a paternal aunt, and had no jobs. Things were hard. They had to start life over from scratch.

As I watched all this happen from my home in Belgium, it tore me apart and felt like torture. For months, I found it hard to sing. Nothing seemed to be worth it. My dad had died, my mother and brother had to leave everything behind and live in a new country with no jobs. Uncertainty became the norm, and I was unable to sing for a year. It killed me to see my mother living her life in this way. But somehow, I found a way to pull myself together. I started singing again.

Throughout my life, my parents always backed me. For most of my adult life, I lived abroad, and nearly all of my performances were in countries other than Syria. Whenever my dad read anything about me in the newspapers, he clipped it and kept it in his pocket, and he was always ready to show it to his friends. These days, I am living in Belgium, and my parents are no longer with me. And when the sadness returns, I feel a responsibility to pull myself together, rise to the occasion, and start singing again. I have discovered that I cannot live without art. I must continue singing and show who I am, as well as what my country and culture is. I am an Armenian

Syrian. I want to share my culture, art, and history with the rest of this world. I will never lower my standards but instead, stand firm. My life began in Syria, and I must make sure that Syria stays with me and becomes part of what I share with others.

One of the most edifying experiences I have had recently was during the summer of 2017, when I participated in a new Spanish festival in La Donaira, a stunning mountainous setting just outside of Málaga. The festival is called Pause, and while attending, I took part in the performances with other international artists known as the Partitura Movement. The Pause festival explores the relationship of humans with music and nature. It is a venue to disconnect from technology and the stressors of everyday life, and is meaningful for the way it allows all participants to share their passion for nature and culture with international musicians. Pause is all about peace, escape, and relaxation.

I would love to go to Syria, especially to Damascus, so that I could visit the conservatory and help young singers flourish. I also yearn to visit my hometown, Aleppo, where I have all my childhood memories. I hope one day this war will end, and I will be able to revisit Syria.

Talar Dekrmanjian
(Credit: Unknown)

CHAPTER 9

We Were Called Heroes
Sarah Mardini (Germany)

———•◦•———

Sarah Mardini was born in Damascus. She became a nationally known prominent figure in swimming in Syria at a young age. Later, as a teenager, her swimming skills saved her own life and the lives of others when she crossed the Mediterranean on a raft. Her journey from Syria to Germany at a young age shaped the way she understands the world, and she has emerged as an internationally renowned refugee and human rights activist. She lives with her family and is currently a student at Bard College in Berlin.

———•◦•———

We Were Called Heroes: Sarah Mardini (Germany)

I was born in Damascus on July 17, 1995. My mother, Mervat, was a physiotherapist, and my dad, Ezzat, was a swimming coach. Both encouraged me to take up swimming, especially my dad—swimming was his life. Beginning when I was five years old, we would go swimming every day. Dad would take me to the pool, and I would spend hours there. After a while, I became hooked, and with lots of practice, became a national competitive swimmer.

My younger sister, Yusra, followed in my footsteps. We both dedicated our lives to swimming from an early age. We were all happy living in Syria.

The civil war broke out in Syria in 2011, and by 2012, my hometown was in a horrendous state. The number of casualties was enormous. My family and I were forced to flee and move to a safer place. Needless to say, as all of this was happening, we stopped training and going to swimming classes. Our entire existence was focused on survival and making it from one day to the next. We lived this way for a full two years.

By 2015, my sister Yusra and I made the decision to leave Syria. We wanted to swim again, study and go to college, live freely, and pursue our dreams. At first, my parents refused to discuss the matter with us. Ideally, we wanted the whole family to go, but that was very risky. Despite their initial trepidation, my parents finally gave in. They let my sister and I leave first. The idea was that they and my youngest sister would join us later. It was an incredibly difficult decision for them to make.

Yusra and I started to make preparations for our escape. We flew to Lebanon and then headed to Turkey. Once we were in Turkey, we met with a smuggler who was ultimately the one who took us across the sea. We were not alone. We were just two of a large group of refugees who were all looking to leave Turkey. But escape was not easy, and we were forced to hide out in a forest near the shore. After spending days there without food, the smuggler gathered us one afternoon at sunset and loaded us onto a dinghy. There were twenty of us, including my dad's two cousins and one of his friends. My sister Yusra and I had our phones, flip flops, and a pair of jeans in our backpacks. That was it! We left Syria with what we had on our backs, and nothing else.

We sailed towards Lesbos, a Greek island close to Turkey. It usually takes about forty-five minutes to navigate there, but after about twenty minutes, the boat's motor suddenly gave out. We were in the middle of the Mediterranean Sea in the dark, at night. We all started to panic. The boat faltered and began to sink.

I instinctively jumped into the water, followed by Yusra, and started pulling the boat towards the shore. We held onto the ropes of the boat with one arm and dragged it through the water with our other arm, kicking all the while. Yusra kept looking at another passenger, a young Iraqi boy. It was clear he was scared. My sister started to make funny faces at him while we were swimming in the cold water. The surf was rough, and the salty water stung our eyes, but we persevered. A couple of other passengers joined us as well, and after about three and half hours, we finally reached Lesbos.

We were happy to make it to shore. In our struggle for survival, my sister and I lost our shoes in the water, and so we were barefoot. A Greek girl approached us and gave Yusra a pair of shoes, and one of the men on the dinghy offered another pair to me. We were extremely exhausted and hungry, and we sought food from local restaurants and businesses. After few hours we ate at a local restaurant. They welcomed us graciously. It is true that we survived the civil war in Syria, but the journey that came after was almost more arduous. We went by foot and train from Lesbos to Greece, Macedonia, Serbia, Hungary, and Austria, and finally reached Germany after an excruciating journey. At one point along the way, we hid for hours in a cornfield at the Serbia-Hungary border. My sister and I got detained by the Hungarian police because we were trying to flee by train to Germany. They sent us to a detention camp in Hungary but we fled and made it to Austria. When we got there, we felt welcomed: we were given teddy bears, shampoo, and other things we needed. After that, we were able to make the last leg of the journey to Germany. Overall, it took us twenty-five days.

Yusra and I reached Berlin on September 7, 2015. We stayed in a refugee camp for eight months. One of the first things we did while there was find a swimming club. An Egyptian translator who was working in the camp put us in contact with Wasserfreunde Spandau 04, and it was there that my sister and I met Sven Spannekrebs, the swim coach. We both started pursuing professional swimming classes, and now Yusra wants to go to the Tokyo Olympics in 2020. Unfortunately, I got a permanent injury and had to stop swimming.

At the end of the eight months, we finally left and got an apartment of our own. Shortly after moving there, I received a message one day on my Facebook page from Erik Gerhardsson, a Swedish volunteer with ERCI (Emergency Response Centre International). He told me he was impressed with our story—we were an inspiration to them. He said that he had also heard our story from children living on Lesbos. He called us heroes.

As soon as this happened, I decided to join the ERCI volunteers in Lesbos. Going back there was hard. Every early morning on the shore reminded me of the perilous night I had spent months before. It was sad and nerve-racking to see desperate people arriving at Lesbos by boat every day.

While all this was going on, the rest of my family made it out of Syria. They went to Berlin too. They now live there in a house where I share a room with my sister.

I spent a year and four months doing volunteer work in Greece. I will be going back to Germany and start going to university. I was granted a full scholarship to Bard College in Berlin. I was thrilled to receive this, and will attend the Law and Medical School. I am an avid human and refugee rights activist, and a public speaker. I have spoken at the UN General Assembly in New York and all over Europe. And I continue to remain focused on my studies. After I graduate from Bard, my dream is to attend Harvard Law School.

I hope my story of hope and courage will change the perception of who the refugees are in this world.

Sarah Mardini
(Credit: Sarah Mardini)

CHAPTER 10

Bread for Bread
Alaa Alhariri (Portugal)

Alaa Alhariri is a native of Damascus who is studying architecture in Lisbon, Portugal. In 2014, she moved from Turkey to Portugal after winning the Jorge Sampaio scholarship for Syrian refugee students. Like most migrants, she struggled to adapt to the culture of her newly adopted home. Alaa discovered that one of the most basic features of all cultures—food—could be the means to open herself up to those around her.

I am a native of Damascus, Syria. I am studying architecture in Lisbon thanks to a scholarship I received from the Jorge Sampaio Global Platform for Syrian Students. I was twenty-one years old when I first got to Lisbon. My journey was not easy: I fled from Syria to Lebanon, then to Egypt, then Turkey, and finally made it to Portugal. At the time (2014), I couldn't speak Portuguese; I only spoke French and Turkish. Communicating with the locals was tough. And while I am entirely grateful for the kind support I received from the Portuguese people, I have to say that they had some problematic ideas about the Syrian people. For example, they asked me if we did our daily commute by camel; if we had electricity; or if all women wore head scarves. The Portuguese had fixed ideas about Middle Easterners, and I had to explain and clarify our multilayered culture and rich traditions. It was challenging to be in Portugal, where people knew so little about Middle Easterners. Mundane chores became hard. Because I did not speak the language, I did not know where to go to buy food or see a doctor, or how to complete paperwork. I had no friends or family. There is nothing more difficult than trying to make a living in a place where you don't speak the language and feel misunderstood.

After I had been in Portugal for about a year, I found that awareness and interest in the Syrian migration grew exponentially because of the sensational news that everyone saw on television: the tragic image of the three-year-old boy Aylan Kurdi, dead on the shores of Greece, victim of a failed migration by boat. At that point, people wanted to help Syrians. Lisbon has its economic issues, but at the same time, people felt the urge to help.

When I moved to Lisbon to enter the university, I had to decide if I wanted to live with a host family or at the university. In my culture, we are used to the idea of privacy in our household, and I always had my own room. The notion of a Middle Eastern girl living with a family other than her own was entirely alien. But I knew that I wanted to learn the language and culture of the Portuguese people, so I decided to live with a family. It was the right move for me. I learned so much: not just the language, but also the cultural mind-set. And just as I learned from them, they too showed curiosity about Syrians. I am a Muslim woman, and that was foreign to them. They were curious to learn about my religion and habits, and about what my life was like back in Syria. This type of exchange helped me integrate into Portuguese society.

One day, a group of Portuguese acquaintances invited me out to a birthday dinner party. We were chatting informally, and one of the people attending asked what it was that I missed the most. I looked around the table and said: "Bread! Syrian bread." For me, bread is the essential element of the Middle Eastern meal. In Middle Eastern culture, bread symbolizes sharing. People pass bread to one another, they break it and share it with each other. We dip our bread into most of our food and then swallow it, rather than using forks. Bread was the thing that reminded me most of my family and home. When I was in Turkey, I noticed that many Syrians opened bakeries and sold Syrian-style bread. It was very popular with both the Turks and Syrians living there.

My attachment to food is something that resonated with Francesca Henriques, a local journalist, as well as Nuno Mesquita and Rita Melo of the social project consultancy Blindesign. Francesca and I began thinking about how we could make Middle Eastern dishes in Portugal and create job opportunities for refugees. Ideally, we'd open a restaurant that served mezze—small plates that are usually shared at the start of a meal. We thought this project could connect Syrian refugees to their roots and make the distance to home feel less than it was. Beyond that, such a plan would expose Portuguese people to a part of the richness of our culture. People here would try these dishes and get a better sense of who we were.

We started networking, and by Christmas, we were preparing dinners at a market called Santa Clara. They were a huge hit. We had young Syrian men and women cooking the food and served roughly one hundred meals a day. People were coming to the market specifically to eat Middle Eastern food. Our food was made fresh daily, and we prepared the table and made people eat just as we did in the Middle East. We made basalieh, kabsa, hummus, baba ganoush. The women who cooked had never worked outside their homes, but they took care of their families, including having cooked and fed them with love, and thus were very well prepared to undertake this task. Most of the men who worked there were in their twenties, and it was an excellent opportunity for them to find employment and learn how to cook. These young men were school-aged at the start of the war and, as a result, had seen their education interrupted. Now, in a new country, they had the opportunity to work, learn a new profession, and go back to school. There was no doubt: we were successful, so the time came to start thinking about establishing a new restaurant where these Syrian women and young men could cook and serve the food.

In mid-March 2016, the Association Pão a Pão (which means "Bread for Bread") was established. That was when Rita Melo and Nuno Mesquita joined us. With the help of the Câmara Municipal de Lisboa, the Alto Comissariado para as migrações, and Turismo de Portugal, we were able to offer restaurant hospitality training at the Escola de Hotelaria de Lisboa (School of Hospitality of Lisbon).

We all worked hard. I volunteered my time for this essentially full-time job, in addition to my studies. We received twenty-three thousand dollars from a crowd-sourcing fund-raising effort, and got a lot of positive coverage in the media. Combined with a bit of luck, we opened Mezze in July 2017. The restaurant employs between twelve and fifteen refugees from Syria, Palestine, and Iraq. Besides food, we have cultural venues including gastronomy workshops, language and debate evenings, and Arabic film screenings. Our goal is to connect with people who have been through hell and back, and thus, can see the value of small things in life.

While most of the refugees headed to Germany, some of us are in Lisbon. And not only Syrians, but Iraqis and Yazidis as well. Job opportunities are scarce in Portugal, and it makes me wonder whether these refugees will be able to stay in Lisbon if they can't find employment.

I am not doing this project to become famous. We Syrians have suffered, and we are still suffering, whether we are in Syria or abroad. I believe that if I can volunteer and, in some way, help alleviate that suffering, I need to do it! Mezze has become part of who I am, but I still plan on continuing with my studies and obtaining my degree in architecture.

Alaa Alhariri
(Credit: Alaa Alhariri)

CHAPTER 11

#EVERYCHILDISMYCHILD
Mirna Kassis (Italy)

Mirna Kassis is a Syrian singer (mezzo-soprano), born in Damascus. She began singing at a very young age, learned both the Arabic and Byzantine musical traditions, and later earned a bachelor's degree in opera singing at the Damascus Conservatory. In 2011, just as the war was breaking out in Syria, she entered a master's degree program in opera singing in Italy. Mirna has performed concerts of both operatic and traditional Arabic music in Syria and other countries. She has become involved in aid work for Syrian refugees and Arab families in Italy, providing language and cultural instruction to migrants. She uses her platform as a performer to raise funds and awareness about the refugee crisis, including participating in a successful series of concerts throughout 2017 (#EVERYCHILDISMYCHILD). She currently lives in Genoa, Italy.

———◆———

بالقلب رح تبقى بسمة صغيرة
تنده لفجر جديد
مليان بالحب
ويحمل امن وسلام

In the heart,
A faint smile will remain
Thirsty to a new Aurora
Filled with love,
And it holds safety and peace.
—Mirna Kassis

———◆———

I was born in Damascus, where I started singing in church at a very young age. At that time, I was introduced to Byzantine chants. My parents encouraged me to learn both Arabic and sacred music, and soon after I started that, I learned about the different melodic modes in traditional music: Maqamaat (oriental scales) and Muwashaat, the names for both Arabic poetic form and a secular genre of music. I started attending a private music institute, and was an active performer at many venues throughout Syria. I have sung as a solo performer since the age of fourteen, and was a chorus member both within, and outside of, the Higher Institute of Music. After I received my baccalaureate (the international equivalent of a high school diploma in the U.S.), I began my university studies with a concentration in archeology. However, I loved singing and kept taking classes alongside my university studies. I was eighteen years old when I met Victor Babenko, an inspiring instructor and conductor from Russia. When he heard my mezzo-soprano voice, he told me that I should focus on studying classical opera singing as I had a suitable voice to sing this repertoire. I entered the Damascus Conservatory and quickly found success as a performer. As both a solo performer and member of the chorus, I performed a wide range of pieces, including Mozart's *Requiem,* Pergolesi's, Dvorak's and Vivaldi's *Stabat Mater,* Beethoven's *Ninth Symphony,* and *Mahler's Kindertotenlieder.* I completed my bachelor's degree in 2011, and then traveled to Italy to attend master classes with Gloria Scalchi. The following year I was admitted to the Conservatorio Niccolò Paganini in Genoa, Italy. Scalchi encouraged me to stay in Italy and study. She encouraged me, and while studying with her, I began to perform on my own, as well as in critical operatic roles at famous theatres in Italy and Europe.

In the meantime, other people were encouraging me to sing oriental music as well. Italians were curious about oriental music. At first, I sang a few short pieces at different venues, and one day was invited to sing at the extraordinary music center Auditorium Parco della Musica in Rome. As I was doing this, I was acutely aware of the fact that even though I was having personal success, I was not doing much to help my fellow stressed-out Syrians. Every time I was on stage and performed oriental music, I felt uncomfortable. I wanted to help them but couldn't find the means to support the Syrian community.

At the outbreak of the war, there weren't many refugees in Genoa, but soon families and children, many with health issues, began to arrive. At once I felt compelled to help, and knew that I could aid in translating from Arabic into Italian. The Syrian families that arrived needed a lot of help—what started as volunteer work became my part-time job as I had to work with them more than four hours a day. Because I travel a lot for my concerts, I often help them by phone.

SPRAR (the Protection System for Asylum Seekers and Refugees) secures accommodation, provides food vouchers, and assists in giving people access to social, health, and educational services. The program also includes an orientation program for refugees, focused on providing information on the best way to find employment and enroll in job training and retraining.

The Pediatric Hospital in Genoa, one of the foremost children's hospitals in Europe, houses the Istituto Giannina Gaslini. The facility had admitted many severely-ill Syrian children who had arrived from Lebanon and Jordan. Many of them were infected with the HIV virus, or had leukemia and other types of cancer. I spent as much time as I could at the hospital even when I was attending classes, performing opera in Holland and Switzerland, attending workshops in Germany, or participating in a weekly program that staged baroque music at historic sites.

I did as much as I could for the Syrian community, and was not alone in my efforts. Many Italian families donated money anonymously to help Syrian and other Arab children. I became very attached to two young children who were suffering from severe illnesses. I found a new passion in teaching Italian to Syrian families.

There was one family, in particular, that was illiterate—they could not even read or write in Arabic—yet they started to learn Italian. I was able to teach them writing and speaking in one year with the help of an Italian instructor. It gave me great satisfaction. I started to help mothers who had dedicated themselves exclusively to taking care of their families and did not work outside their house when they were in Syria. Here they needed help understanding Italian society and culture. Many of them had to work for the first time in their lives outside the house.

In the summer of 2017, an Italian actress named Anna Foglietta launched a new initiative called Every Child is my Child. It included the support of over 250 names that included actors, musicians, television personalities, and sports figures. Directors planned series of performances where all profits would go towards well-vetted causes. The first goal was to raise funds together with ONLUS (organizzazione Non Lucrativa di Utilità Sociale), an Italian social organization. "Together You Can Do Something" was a performance staged to benefit the Plaster School, a small primary school in Reyhanli, Turkey, which sits on the border of Syria and Turkey. Funds were earmarked for medical care and food. I was invited to join the fabulous production and sang with world-renowned singers, as we raised awareness for Syrian refugees. It was a joyful and fulfilling experience.

At last, I was able to help my fellow Syrians and bring awareness to their plight at a major international venue. As a bonus, my efforts were recognized, and I was awarded a prize on *Tú sí que vales*, an Italian television show. On November 3, 2017, we had another spectacular performance—you can follow all the initiative's news at www.everychildismychild.it.

My wish is for equality and peace in this world, and that all borders disappear so each person can travel freely and meet others. On a personal level, my wish is for all arms to vanish, and peace for Syria, so kids grow up with a normal childhood—a fundamental right in our society.

Mirna Kassis
(Credit: UNHCR Italia)

CHAPTER 12

Gabriele, the Luthier
Gabriele Jebran Yakoub (Germany)

Gabriele Jebran Yakoub was born in Russia and raised in Damascus, Syria. As the son of a professional cellist, he began studying music at a young age and, despite recognition from prominent musicians, he abandoned becoming a professional musician to pursue violin making. He moved from Syria to Cremona, Italy to be in the center of the most highly regarded luthier tradition. After studying there, he now calls on his unique Syrian and Russian heritages to craft instruments that combine the quality of the highest-end violins with signature artistic details. He currently lives in Berlin.

I am the first internationally-known Syrian violin maker in the world. I left Syria when I was seventeen years old and went to Cremona, Italy, a small city that does not have an orchestra. The population is around 65,000, and most of the people who live there work in agriculture. However, it is also renowned as an excellent center for violin making. Moving to Cremona represented a significant risk for me because there are almost four hundred violin makers located there but no professional musicians. Most of the violin makers are from well-known families that have been in the business for generations. I am not the first Arab violin maker—that title belongs to Marco Dobretsovich. He was born in Dulcigno, Montenegro, and studied with Pollastri in Bologna in the 1920s. Dobretsovich moved to Egypt, married an Egyptian woman, and established himself in both Alexandria and Cairo. He died in 1957 and is still known as the first violin maker in the Arab world.

Making violins is a challenging career for a Syrian. I was fifteen years old and living in Syria when I decided to follow this path. I was fascinated with science, jewelry, and music. Violin making brings these things together. My mother was a professional cellist who graduated from St. Petersburg (Russia) with a doctorate. My father was a hydrogeological engineer, who studied at the oldest geological institute in St. Petersburg, founded by Catherine the Great. When he finished his studies, he decided to move to Syria. He was a communist and an honest person, who never stole a cent and was very modest. My mother was the opposite: she did not believe in communism. The two of them lived in Russia during Brezhnev's time in office and things there were terrible. By the time they decided to move, the war in Lebanon had started, and I was two years old.

At first, we moved to Qamishli. People only spoke Kurdish and Aramaic there, and my parents did not know either of these languages. Once my father got a job in the Ministry of Irrigation, we moved to Damascus. My mother joined the Chamber Music Orchestra, led by Solhi Al-Wadi. Soon after, she started to teach at the Higher Institute of Music. My mother's first job had been working at the opera studio in St. Petersburg as a professional cellist. So of course, I grew up taking cello lessons.

During my youth, I spent much more time with my mother than my father, studying music and attending classes at school. Whenever I was with my father, I was fascinated by his maps, and his knowledge of chemistry and physics. My mother wanted me to become a cellist. I studied very methodically and played the cello very well, and earned my Baccalaureate in playing the cello. However, I did not feel that I had the true calling for being a professional cellist. Every summer we traveled and always stopped in St. Petersburg. I listened to, and even met, many of the famous musicians there; compared to them, I found my skills lacking. I could play the cello well and read music competently, but compared to the Russians, I was not proficient enough. They read, understood, and analyzed music like a conductor and had a flair for performance. These are skills that young people learn at the Russian institutions. Rostropovich, Barenboim, Gergiev, and many other prominent musicians knew me as a cellist, but I decided I wanted a career in violin making rather than as a cellist playing in an orchestra.

When I got to Cremona, I had a Syrian name: Jebran Yakoub. I was unlike all the others, who had Italian family names, or those who had adapted Italian names once they became luthiers. I was unknown to them. I sign my violins as Jebran Yakoub, my Syrian name, and on the inside, I write Gabriele Jebran Yakoub, because my mother used to call me Gabriel.

In 1997 I won the violin-making competition in Russia and went back to Damascus. I was interested in creating a logo or symbol as a brand for my violin, so I started to search. At the same time, I began working in the workshop at the Bachoura family jewelry store Bab Tuma. Combining my fascination with Fabergé designs from the Hermitage in St. Petersburg with my background in Syrian jewelry design, I started creating violin pegs with gold and gilded frames, as well as others that were encrusted with diamonds or other precious stones. Both my Syrian and Russian backgrounds inspired me to make violins with unique designs. My teacher in St. Petersburg was Vladimir Kitov. He taught me the art of making Fabergé embellishments. I dedicated my Royal Mastery pegs to him. We came up with the idea of making these pegs together while at the Hermitage on my birthday in 2015. Sadly, he has since passed on.

My unique designs were successful on their own, and I sell my violins all over the world. When I was living in Cremona, my mother called me often to check on me and see if I needed money, but I never took any money from my parents. I worked and was living life independently—I had a free soul. I built my empire alone. Now I have many admirers and steady work, creating new violins.

When I look back, I see that there is no tradition of making violins in my family. My great-grandfather, Isaichev Matvej Mikhailovich, was a military economist and the one who called for the evacuation of St. Petersburg after the blockade of the city during World War II. He had started off as a military officer in the tsar's White Army, and during the Russian Revolution, the Red Army asked him to join forces with them. My great-grandmother was a believer. She kept her icons hidden in the bathroom and prayed to them secretly during those times. My mother was the first professional cellist in the family. I carry a Syrian passport, but I don't feel very Syrian myself. I travel the world and meet renowned musicians and intellectuals from all over the globe. Right now, I reside in Berlin and work diligently, though I love my summer voyages to the Greek islands. I try to enjoy every moment of my life and cherish it with people I care about.

Gabriele Jebran Yakoub
(Credit: Evgeny Evtyukhov)

CHAPTER 13

Dalya, The Teenager
Dalya Zeno (United States)

D alya Zeno was born in Aleppo and fled Syria in 2012 at the beginning of the country's uprising. In 2017, she was featured in Julia Meltzer's documentary *Dalya's Other Country*. The film tells the story of members of a family displaced by the Syrian conflict and shows how they reestablished themselves in the United States. The importance of the mother-daughter relationship was a core theme. The documentary also follows Dalya through the politically volatile period of Donald Trump's election. She currently lives in Los Angeles and studies Business at Pasadena City College.

In 2012, shortly after the Syrian uprising started, I left Aleppo with my mother, and we fled to Los Angeles. Back then, I thought we would return to Syria within a short period. But there was no way we could return. We were lucky enough to have U.S. citizenship already (see below). In fact, before we moved here, I would visit every summer with my family. Unlike most Syrians, we did not have to cross the Mediterranean on a raft, but similar to them, we struggled with the loss of our home and found it hard to fit into American culture.

I enrolled at Holy Family High School, an all-girls Catholic school. At first, life in the U.S. was very hard for me. I had to adjust to many different things. For example, I was the only girl wearing a hijab in a Catholic school. Everybody was curious about it, and they wanted to know why I was wearing it. But actually, those questions became good conversational topics, and people started to let me in as a friend.

Everyone at my school was open-minded. Many students came from minority backgrounds, so there were challenges in life that we shared. I was blessed to be there. It was a small school, and everyone knew each other. I grew up there and had many positive experiences. I learned from my classmates. I participated in sports, dance, and other artistic activities at school, and I think that if I had gone to a public school, it would have been harder for me to do all of this. I was already firmly grounded in my Islamic religious upbringing. However, my mother was concerned about the peer pressure I would experience from American society. For my mother, going out with friends, having a boyfriend, coming home late, and wearing inappropriate clothes were all critical issues.

Dalya, The Teenager: Dalya Zeno (United States)

Middle Eastern values are different from American ones. Finding a balance between the two was a challenge for my mom and me, including attending a private school rather than a large public one. She thought it would be easier for the two of us to adjust to life in the U.S. Peer pressure is always an issue, but at a Catholic school, the community is small, and there are many rules. In this context, an environment where teachers engaged with students all helped to make life more manageable.

I loved the Catholic high school I attended because it taught me to be humble and open-minded. I had to live outside my comfort zone, and it allowed me to integrate into American society slowly. It was an eye-opening experience. I am now able to leave my house and be empathetic toward others, putting myself in their shoes. I do this with every person I speak to: I imagine myself in their situation, because if I do not, I may not be able to discover the kindness that lies within them. Understanding and respect are reciprocal.

During my high school years, my brother was working with a film production company, and they wanted to make a documentary about our life in the U.S. I was in high school and trying to fit in, and one day they walked into my school with a camera. I was so embarrassed to be in front of a camera at school. I did not want them to be there, but I got used to it as time went by. That footage culminated in *Dalya's Other Country*.

My mother was also a big part of the film. She is a brave woman and was recently accepted at UCLA. My brother Mustafa and I are so proud of her. She is divorced and just graduated from community college, where she majored in business administration. She will continue her studies at UCLA, where she will study to get her bachelor's degree in Arabic and Islamic Studies. My parents lived here before, in 1982. After they got married, my mom joined my dad in the U.S. Both of my brothers were born here, but ultimately a few years later my parents decided to go back to Syria. My mother then decided to return to the U.S. after the war broke out in Syria. Back in Syria, she did not have to work; here, she has to work, as well as study. In the U.S., no one has time to even breathe! It is hard to find time to see family or friends because everyone is in a rush and busy. Back in Syria, people had the time to enjoy friends and family.

After I graduated from high school and moved on to college, I found it hard to adjust again, especially during the first semester. Up until that point, in the U.S., the only thing I knew was my high school, which I considered my second home. I loved and knew everyone there on a personal level. When I graduated, each one of us had to go off in our own direction. It was a familiar feeling for me. It was like leaving Syria and coming to the U.S. all over again. Being alone and trying to fit in and adjusting to a new environment was tough, but now I love it. I am well-adjusted and in my second year of studies, focusing on business.

My father lives in Turkey, and I am trying to volunteer there at a Syrian refugee camp when I have the time. I miss my dad, and this would be a way for me to see him and help with the refugee crisis.

I live in L.A., and I am privileged not to feel the Islamophobia that much of the rest of the country does. My hijab serves as a reminder of who I am, and what my values, morals, and beliefs are. It is part of my identity. Wearing it has also helped me to have empathy and use my kind personality to challenge people's perceptions of Muslims.

Dalya Zeno
(Credit: Asmaa Tabban)

CHAPTER 14

Aleppo, A Walking Museum
Kevork Mourad (United States)

Kevork Mourad is a Syrian-Armenian artist born in the Syrian town of Qamishli and raised in Aleppo. He is well-known for his paintings and visual compositions and has been featured as a solo artist at the Contemporary Art Platform in Kuwait; he has also been part of collaborative exhibitions such as the 2010 Liverpool Biennial and the 2014 Art Moment in Budapest, Hungary. He is also well-known for his collaboration with other artists, such as Yo-Yo Ma's Silk Road Ensemble; Kinan Azmeh, composer and clarinetist; Anaïs Tekerian, the singer and writer; and Issam Rafea, the composer. Kevork currently resides in New York City.

———•———

I am a Syrian-Armenian artist, born in 1970 in the small town of Qamishli, Syria. I am known mostly for my paintings, which I make spontaneously in collaboration with musicians, dancers, and composers. I grew up in Aleppo in a very low-income family. I did not have any toys of my own; I had to make them and create my own games. Aleppo did not have recreational parks, playgrounds, or public libraries. Pencil and paper were my best toys. My teachers and classmates in elementary school encouraged me to become an artist when they saw my drawings, and by the age of six, I had already decided to pursue art as a career. At school, I had two teachers who were also artists, and they helped me nurture my love of art. I spent a lot of time in their studios, as well as in the school's library, where I found refuge in books. By the time I was fourteen years old, I was making money selling my drawings to printing shops.

My parents were not very educated, and did not approve of my interest in pursuing art. However, I somehow found the courage to apply for the opportunity to study abroad and attended school in Armenia. I received my master's in fine arts from the Yerevan State Academy of Fine Arts, and in 1998 was lucky enough to be able to begin my career in the U.S. after being sponsored by an American philanthropist. For me, Syria is my home. It is the origin of my memories—I long for the culture because it's what defines me as an artist. The U.S. is the place where I evolved as an artist and was able to build my own family, with my wife and two daughters. In a sense, it has become my real home.

In my early works I was mostly inspired by the idea of migration and deportation because, like many Armenian artists, I thought a great deal on the Armenian Genocide. I work with three media: painting on paper, color on canvas, and performance on video. Painting on paper is like a sound: it keeps resonating on, and I do not erase its lines. I apply black paint (acrylic or ink) without having the option of deleting it. I have created a custom-made tool for squeezing and smudging the paint that I use throughout all my work. When I work on canvas, I mostly use acrylic, because I like the idea of creating paintings that are layered. Once I have a composition in mind, I usually put down the abstract colors as a base and then build layers of calligraphic black lines. This goes on, over and over, by alternating the black lines and the color. As for the video-performance pieces, I create both live and pre-animated pieces. Sometimes I film a dancer and create lines on top of the clip, using a stop-motion animation technique. In principle, music and politics profoundly influence all my animated pieces.

When I moved to New York, I met the wonderful Syrian composer and clarinetist Kinan Azmeh. I had always loved music and saw a lot of promise in collaborating with him. We started to work together by incorporating music with audiovisuals, and created several projects. I have also collaborated with many other artists, such as Yo-Yo Ma and the Silk Road Ensemble, and have been featured all over the world, from Mexico City to Japan, throughout the U.S. and across Europe. My latest venue was in Los Angeles at the Walt Disney Concert Hall, for a new production of Handel's *Israel in Egypt* oratorio. This performance was part of the Los Angeles Master Chorale and Grant Gershon's Hidden Handel project. It featured eighty singers, seven soloists, and an orchestra enhanced by my compelling mix of drawings, animation, and film as I created imagery in real-time from the stage during the performance. I was able to bring my perspective to this work's universal theme of displacement and the nature inherent in humans to return home. With *Israel in Egypt*, I highlighted parallels between the exodus of Israelites and the plagues which surrounded Egypt, as presented in the libretto, with today's forced migrants' experiences. I have no other option than to express in my creations the need for unity and the reality of human suffering, which are the same wherever you go.

As an artist growing up in Aleppo, the city was a walking museum. It's an old city, with ancient arches, porticoes, and doorways that have Roman, Byzantine, Islamic, and Hellenic styles. Cities and towns in Syria have a multilayered history. It is a complete sensory experience: the sounds of children playing in the streets, pigeons cooing, peddlers crying out to passersby, minarets calling the faithful to prayer, and churches ringing their bells. Everything fed my eyes and ears, and this is all reflected in my art. Telling the story of this society with its past and present is the central theme of my art. This includes the forced migration of Syrians and their stories. I feel that as an artist I should be a witness to my society and document their lives. In my art, I love creating a diary of the events of my homeland. Over four hundred thousand people have died in the Syrian uprising, and more than 6.5 million were displaced. Syria, a multicultural country, has been impoverished and fractured. Loss and devastation are everywhere. My art aims to celebrate my rich cultural heritage even as I mourn its loss.

I left Syria a long time ago, and my life with my American family is rooted in New York. But I always dream of having a studio in Damascus, because it inspires me more than any other place in this world.

Kevork Mourad
(Credit: Ed Tadevossian)

CHAPTER 15

Maya, The Woman in Progress
Maya Shahaf (Sweden)

M aya Shahaf was born in Damascus, where she also received her bachelor's degree in English Literature. Her compelling story of a mother and a woman living in Dubai, and now Sweden, demonstrates the refugee family journey.

———•———

In 2011 my husband, George Oro, and I left Syria and started to work in Doha. George is a musician who worked at Qatar Foundation, and I worked at Cornell University as an assistant to the Dean of Administration. I gained a lot of experience working those few months. I was supposed to be tenured, but due to the political turmoil between Syria and Qatar at that time, they deferred me. Instead, I held a new position at Qatar University, working at the School of Law as a Business Coordinator. In Syria, I studied English Literature and for five years worked promoting and selling higher education textbooks for SEP, a franchise of Librairie du Liban Publishers in Syria, and after that worked for a year at the Bank of Syria and Overseas. As a Syrian, it was hard to find stability in the Gulf. We were always conscious of our identity and realized that at any time we could be asked to leave Doha.

By 2014, when I was pregnant, we had made the decision to leave. We had to plan our future. If we were asked to leave Doha, our only choice was to go back to Syria, where my husband would have to fulfill his military service obligation. The situation in Syria was terrible. Considering all these circumstances we applied to get visas to the U.S. and Europe. We were lucky enough to get both. I felt spoiled to have two options. Not many Syrians had this opportunity. Between the U.S. and Sweden, we chose Sweden. In the meantime, my husband's parents had left Syria and went to Sweden. George is from Qamishli, in Syria. Many people from his town were able to leave and live in Sweden. That's why he had many acquaintances in Sweden prior to our move. We decided to go to Sweden and apply for refugee status. I was eight months pregnant when we made it to Sweden; after two days I applied for refugee status. I was united with my in-laws, and Sweden is where my son was born.

My son is four years old now. He goes to nursery and speaks Swedish, English, and Arabic. As a mother and a resident of Sweden, I have three personalities. Maya that speaks Arabic—mother and wife; Maya that speaks English—professional at work;

and Maya that speaks Swedish—mother, colleague, and citizen who communicates with her children and the community. Upon my arrival in Sweden, I spent my first year at home with my newborn son, but once he was ready to go to nursery school, I started intensive Swedish language course classes, and began to look for a job. Now, for two years, I have been working at Viacom International Media Networks as a Nordic Programming Operations Coordinator.

Every day, I have to prove to people that I am a professional in my job, in my career, in relations with my family and others. People have wrong perceptions about Syrians. I am an educated woman, who is fluent in three languages, have a strong work ethic, and am kind, considerate, and gracious in dealing with people and my family. I don't wear the veil, and when we were in Syria, we never lived under tents with camels. I am asked many times if we ate Halal meat. I am a Damascene girl. My father comes from a small town in Deraa which we try to visit occasionally, but in my heart, I belong to the historic and ancient city of Damascus, where I was living, studying, and working.

Many people ask me how could I live in Sweden while my parents and siblings are still in Syria. It's a difficult question to answer. My mother was diagnosed with myeloma and we lost her in August 2017. I was forced to continue living my normal life while the most precious person in my world was suffering and fading far away from me. My father and brother are still in Damascus, as are some of my closest relatives. I speak with them every day, first thing in the morning, and then continue my daily chores. I have a child and a husband to take care of and a job to attend to. I don't watch the news or films of the war. I focus on my responsibilities, so we can live peacefully in Sweden. It's not an easy life knowing your loved ones are living in a war zone, while you're far away. But having a son makes me forget the difficulties of life, even if just for a few minutes. He is my inspiration to live life day-by-day and face all my challenges with patience. I have to survive, deal with daily issues, raise my child, and take care of my family. I thank God every day when the day is over, because it's one more day my family has survived the war.

My husband is a professional musician and he tours a great deal outside of Sweden. He has the freedom to travel to many countries and share his musical talent. Every day, my son goes to school and gets tremendous attention from his teachers. The education system in Sweden is top-notch! I am so happy that my son has such an opportunity. The communication between his school and me is open, and I'm able to use my language skills proficiently.

Recently, I wanted to have a birthday party for my son. Back home, we decide what we're going to serve guests—we don't contact the other parents to see what their preferences are. Here, I had to plan every detail according to what the invited Swedish families and children wanted. It's a simple birthday party for children, but as a newcomer to Sweden, it took a lot of energy and effort. I had to figure out how to contact each parent, and then ask them if their children had any allergies, as well as what kind of food and sweets I should serve. It was a tedious job for a party that lasted just two hours. I had to spend a few days planning and deciding what's the best, most meaningful way to celebrate my son's birthday with his classmates.

Stereotyping exists here. When I want to set up a playdate for my son, I have to approach the families and present myself. Although Swedish families are welcoming, I still feel they are a bit reserved because we are Syrian. It's a daily struggle to fit in without losing our identity. If we were in Syria, it doesn't mean that we would be happier, it just means we would not have these issues. Life would be simpler.

Many people are surprised that I speak several languages, work in a reputable company, and have a family that is thriving. I soon hope to gain admission to college so I can earn my master's in Media and Communication and pursue a higher position within my organization. What bothers me a lot is the preconceptions the Swedish have towards the Syrians. I have to explain many times to people who I am, and tell them there are many Syrians like me who are educated and ambitious. I work hard every day and look forward to having a happy and prosperous life with my loved ones.

Maya Shahaf
(Credit: Maya Shahaf)

CHAPTER 16

Dance or Die

Ahmad Joudeh (The Netherlands)

Ahmad Joudeh was born in Yarmouk Camp for Palestinian refugees, located in Damascus. He became interested in music and performance at a young age, and as a teenager, he gained international acclaim on the Lebanese version of the hit TV show *So You Think You Can Dance*. Ahmad views art as a defiant practice and one that can stand up to the violence that currently engulfs the Syrian territory. He left Syria in 2016 and now works as a professional dancer based in Amsterdam.

———◈———

I grew up with music. Art was part of my home environment. I would sing along with my father, who was an accordion player and painter. My brother played the oud (lute), my sister, the violin, and all of us played around on the keyboard. My dad taught music out of our home. My childhood was full of music and art. All of this took place within the refugee camp.

My first artistic memory from outside the home happened when I was eight years old, and sang in the choir at Yarmouk, an unofficial refugee camp in Damascus. I saw some students dancing *Swan Lake*. I remember thinking that the flute's tune was angelic and was mesmerized: I started to sway and dance along with the sounds. And then I began to wonder about whether I wanted to sing, or dance. I asked my father again and again: "Why can't I play the keyboard and move at the same time?" I started to listen to music on my own, and I would secretly dance behind locked doors. As I grew older and became a teenager, my voice grew deeper and lost its charm. By 14, it was clear that I was not meant to become a singer. As this was happening, I started to secretly attend professional dance classes at the Higher Institute for Music in Damascus. I studied dance, choreography, lighting, and other subjects, and I danced with the Inanna Dance Group.

My mother always encouraged me to dance. She knew what she was talking about, because she had studied gymnastics. She would watch me when I danced and commented on my posture and movements. But my father was against it. He considered my dancing shameful. He ascribed to the typical masculine, cultural norms of the time and, in fact, would beat me for dancing. But his beatings didn't stop me. I kept on my path. My parents got divorced during my teenage years, and as a result, I was able to dance freely at home.

Dance or Die: Ahmad Joudeh (The Netherlands)

In 2014, I entered the Lebanese version of the television dance competition *So You Think You Can Dance*. During the semifinals, the jury panel told me I could not win because I was Palestinian and, thus, lacked a legitimate nationality. In a word, politics got in the way of my success. Nevertheless, because of the exposure I received on the show, I had thousands of viewers who liked my dancing. I had thousands of followers on social media across the region and around the world.

As all of this was going on, there was escalating tension between Syrian opposition forces and the government; the Yarmouk camp in Damascus, where I lived with my family, was seized in the conflict. At the time, around 160,000 Palestinian refugees were living in the refugee camp. We were all considered "stateless," since this camp existed within Syrian borders and outside the jurisdiction of the Palestinian authority. Yarmouk quickly turned into a premier battleground for fighters. They bombed our house, and my family members were either killed or forced to flee. I lost everything other than what I carried inside of me: dancing. I had nothing from my home, no childhood pictures, no personal belongings, no extra clothes. I wasn't alone: everyone from the camp lost all they had. We were forced out and found shelter with relatives of my mother who lived near the refugee camp. To keep me going, every morning I would go up to the roof and practice my dancing for several hours, then head to dance school.

Our stay there didn't last long. Due to continuing bombings and sieges, my mother was forced to leave her relatives' home, and she decided to move to Palmyra, where her parents lived. I refused to follow her. Instead, I stayed in Damascus so that I could complete my dance exams. While I was preparing for them, I was also teaching dance to young children. Some friends offered me a place to stay. I lived there for a few days but then had to move out. I pitched a tent on the roof of their building and stayed there for two months.

Around that time, I started to receive death threats from the Islamic State because I was dancing, but I did not give up. I kept on dancing. In fact, I got a tattoo on my neck that said "Dance or Die." The tattoo is located precisely where the Islamic State would sink in their knives to cut off my head.

It was during the summer of 2016 when Roozbeh Kaboly, from the Dutch program *Nieuwsuur*, found me on Facebook. He had seen my performances from *So You Think You Can Dance* and wanted to interview me in Syria. He met me in Bab Touma, a borough in Damascus. His first question to me was, "Where do you want to dance?" At the time, I had just graduated and was facing my military service obligation. In Syria, all men must serve in the army for three years, so I told him, "I am getting ready to go into the army. But I have two things to do before I go there. If I go off to the army, I will be there for three years." I did not want to fight, but I had no choice. "Before I head off to the army, I want to go to Yarmouk refugee camp and dance among the rubble. And then, I want to go to Palmyra and dance there too." So, we went there together. ISIS fired on us, but I went anyway. I wanted to prove that I was not afraid. I took my mom too, and we went to Palmyra. She saw her parents' house in ruins. Everything was gone. I danced on the very same stage in Palmyra where ISIS executed its victims. As we did that, Mr. Kaboly filmed me and ultimately created a fifteen-minute documentary about my life called *Dance or Die.*

Immediately, I received dozens of invitations to perform and attend dance institutions and choreography companies around the world. My dream was to go to Amsterdam, and it came true when Ted Brandsen, the artistic director of the Dutch National Ballet, set up the Dance for Peace fund. It was a dream come true. In 2016, I arrived in Amsterdam and entered the Dutch National Ballet. And thankfully, this fund will continue to bring other Syrian dancers and choreographers to the Netherlands in the future.

Dance is a beautiful art form, and I believe that there is a lot of room for growth regarding how we think about it in Arab countries. Where I am from, we have many great dancers, but their art is not respected, and they are not free to express their ideas in the open. For example, my teachers did not let me dance the way I wanted—they did not allow me to explore. The institution dictated the way it wanted us to dance, and this did not let me or other dancers flourish in Syria. Many talented dancers in Syria do not have the opportunity to advance their skills in dancing.

I am the first Arab dancer in a professional dance company in the world. I am a human being alive and well in Amsterdam. I can express all my feelings and thoughts through dance. I use my entire body to express my feelings.

When I was a student in Syria, I got used to being called a refugee. But now, the whole world calls me the "Syrian dancer." And yet, I don't even possess Syrian nationality. Some cynical people say that I took advantage of the Syrian Civil War. But it's not true! I have no identity. I have lived my life in a Palestinian refugee camp. My house was destroyed, and members of my family were killed. I buried my uncle with my own hands, but I still attended dancing school. When I showed up at school and told the principal why I was late, he responded: "You're only allowed to be late when you bury your mother!" I will never forget that. I was doing all that I could to control my feelings. It took everything I had to be the student who fulfilled his obligation to come to class.

While I was in Syria, the government allowed me to choreograph the Youth Cinema and Short Films Festival as well as a performance at the opera house in Damascus. I was pleased to have choreographed the opening dance for the festival in the capital. But things have been stalled for awhile now. I wanted to stay in Syria, but I also wanted to be a dancer and fight for civilization, rather than fight as a soldier. Now I am in Amsterdam and do not need to fight. I have the freedom to express myself, and I have a much clearer vision of my art.

Melancholy is with me every day: I carry sadness or happiness with me daily. Dancing helps me work through this, as my movements vary with my feelings from day to day. I still have students in Syria. I try to be a good example to them in both words and actions. I want them all to have the opportunity to be educated and have the chance to pursue their dreams through hard work. I want them to be able to have faith in life, and have a goal to fulfill. I send money to my students at SOS, a school for Down's Syndrome children. Every month my students send me a video to let me know what they are up to in their creative dance classes.

Dance or Die: Ahmad Joudeh (The Netherlands)

Sending remittances abroad is part of my life. I send money to my mother, my neighbors, other people who need it, and of course, students of dance. My mother still lives in Syria. I check WhatsApp several times a day to make sure that she is OK. If the application is on, I have peace of mind, but if it's not, I immediately get worried. I hope that I will be reunited with my mother, father, and siblings someday.

I am at home with the idea of being a refugee. I was born a refugee, in a camp in Syria. Here is how I see it: we Palestinians are guests wherever we go. Being a guest in another country is similar to being a guest in someone's home. We will leave one day. In the end, we are all refugees.

Right now, I don't even have a passport, but have applied for one. I refuse to live in a refugee camp in Amsterdam. Instead, I work and work towards getting the necessary travel documents I need to perform in different countries. Dancing is my life. I live life to dance.

I will continue to travel to Greece and visit the refugee camps, looking for young talent. It makes sense because once I was living and hiding in a refugee camp.

Syria is home to one of the oldest and most advanced civilizations. Sadly, ISIS has wiped out thousands of years of history in some cities and towns. It is not only the destruction of monuments and buildings; it's also the intangible beliefs and practices related to them and the values given to them. Every time I dance and choreograph my dancing, I unite Syrian and Western cultures. I hope I can continue to dance, dream, and share it all with the rest of the world.

Ahmad Joudeh
(Credit: Marc Driessen)

ABOUT THE AUTHOR

Mimi Melkonian teaches Arabic, French, and "Attack and Aftermath of 9/11" at Brunswick School in Greenwich, Connecticut. She has extensive experience in teaching Arabic language and culture in creative ways in the classroom, as well as online.

She is a frequent presenter at linguistic conferences and seminars in the U.S., Europe, and the Middle East. She is invited annually to present at the Columbia Scholastic Press Association Convention at Columbia University in New York City.

Mimi has been honored with several awards, including the Goodwill Ambassador Award from the Secretary of State and Governor of Arkansas for her valuable contribution to the Little Rock Sister Cities Commission and the IBLA-Little Rock Music Festival. She is a Licentiate of The Institute of Mathematics and its Applications, IMA, in London. In 2017, she was awarded the Educational Technology Award from the American Council on the Teaching of Foreign Languages (ACTFL), an organization that promotes the teaching and learning of Arabic language and culture in the United States. Most recently, in 2018, Mimi was elected secretary for the Arabic Special Group (SIG) at ACTFL.

Index

Index

CRÁTER PUBLISHERS

Ediciones del Cráter

"Painting, but also literature and all that goes with it, is merely a process of going round and round something inexpressible, round a black hole, or a crater, whose center one cannot penetrate. And those things one seizes as subject matter, they have merely the character of pebbles at the foot of the crater–they mark out a circle which, one hopes, draws ever closer to the center."

—Anselm Kiefer

CPSIA information can be obtained
at www.ICGtesting.com
Printed in the USA
BVHW031054020619
549937BV00004B/5/P